DATE DUE

Demco

Tools
for
Time
Management

Christian Perspectives on Managing Priorities

Edward R. Dayton

ZONDERVAN
PUBLISHING HOUSE OF THE ZONDERVAN CORPORATION
GRAND RAPIDS, MICHIGAN 49506

Tools for Time Management
Copyright © 1974 by The Zondervan Corporation
Library of Congress Catalog Card Number 74-4958

This edition 1978
Cloth: ISBN 0-310-23220-1
Paper: ISBN 0-310-23221-X

Printed in the United States of America

CONTENTS

PREFACE

This book is the compilation of some very full years of experience with a variety of secular and Christian organizations. It reflects not only my own thinking, but the thoughts of hundreds of men and women who have considered most of these ideas before me. If I bring anything new to the discussion of life management, it is probably more in the area of Christian integration, rather than new techniques.

But there is nothing here that I have not personally observed or attempted. It's practical. It works. My goal for this book is somehow to loosen the shackles of indecision, overwork, guilt and frustration that burden all leaders, but especially plague the Christian executive.

I can't promise that using the ideas and principles I have described will make you "happier" or even more "successful." Those are not important terms to me. But I think I can offer you a greater peace with yourself, your family, and the tasks God has given you to do. And perhaps — just perhaps — a greater sense of joy at being alive and part of God's wonderful creation.

Two men have had a special impact on me as I have written. Dr. Ted Engstrom (the Executive Vice President of World Vision) and I have spent many hundreds of hours listening to each other as we have team-taught "Managing Your Time" seminars. Ted's strong leadership and personal convictions have had a special place in my thinking.

Dr. Gerald P. Foster is Professor of Administrative Systems and the Business Administration Department at Denver University. He has not only been a consistently good critic of our teaching ("If no one's learning something, why teach it?"), but has done me the honor of patiently critiquing this manuscript. I am deeply grateful.

Edward R. Dayton

INTRODUCTION

This book is like a box of tools: there are some here you won't need, and hopefully some which will be very important to you. This is why the book has been arranged alphabetically, so that you can pick out the ones that you want.

There are a number of ways in which you can use the book:

- You can plunge in any place you want, and select those topics which are useful to you.
- You can start at the beginning and read through.
- You can move from one subject to another by noting the cross-referenced chapter titles, which are always given in capitals. If you are going to start with any chapter, I'd suggest "PEOPLE." That's what life is all about.

You might wonder about the format. It is immediately obvious that the idea comes from R. C. Townsend's *Up The Organization*. I find the *dis*continuity of ideas on the same subject personally stimulating and thought-provoking. I hope you will feel the same.

This book is written from a strong Christian bias, for which I offer no apology. As you can see from the chapter on "Assumptions," I think that a meaningful, full life can only come from an understanding of who I am, why I am here and where I am going. I believe the answers to those questions are found in the person of Jesus Christ.

I am a pragmatic man. To me faith is, as John Carnell put it so well, "The mind's resting in the sufficiency of the evidence." As I have tried to live the life that is Christian, the evidence of God's work at every hand is overwhelming. But that's another book which I'm sure someone else is more qualified to write than I.

So on to discovering how to manage your life which is really managing your time . . .

Tools
for
Time
Management

"Live life then, with a due sense of responsibility, not as men who do not know the meaning and purpose of life but as *those who do*. Make the best use of your time, despite all the difficulties of these days."

Ephesians 5:15, 16
(Phillips)

A, B, C's

What to do next? How to set our priorities straight? Sometimes it's trying to sort out our goals. Sometimes it's just trying to decide which is most important.

When faced with a long list of things to do, most people have difficulty deciding which ones come first, second, third, fourth, etc. Many times the trouble is just trying to decide which is number one. By the time we get to number two, we're exhausted. One way around this is the A, B, C approach to determining priorities.

When you do have a long list of things-to-do, or goals to accomplish, don't try to decide which is best, which is second best, etc. Instead, categorize them. Category "A" may be *very important*, "B" may be *less important*, and "C" may be *least important*. Or again "A" may be *must do* (or *must be!*), "B" may be *should do* (or *be*), and "C" may be *can do* (or *can be*).

First, go through your list and note all the A items, then all the B items, and then all the C items. If a long list of A items remains, then go through all the A items applying your A, B, C's just to the A's.

You'll be surprised at how quickly you'll be able to set things in an acceptable order. A major advantage is that you are not forced to end up with a one, two, three ranking. Many times a number of items will be of equal value. Why insist that one be top dog?

This is an especially effective technique in working with a group. It permits us to quickly write down all the ideas the group has without rejecting any of them. Then the group can sort them out by reaching consensus, not on which is first, second, etc., but rather by categories. You'll be surprised how quickly a group can work this way, and will be pleased with the added bonus afforded by the categories themselves — group self-understanding and precision of purpose. (See GOOD GOALS AND BAD GOALS)

ACCOUNTABILITY

Nothing happens if one doesn't consider himself accountable.

A noted secular psychologist has commented rather cogently on the value of holding one another accountable for our actions. In his view the early church discovered the tremendous social value of confessing our shortcomings to one another. But then the Roman church came along and said we only had to confess our sins to the priest. The Protestants made it worse. They said we only had to confess our sins to God. Then Freud came along and blew the whole thing: he said we didn't have any sins to confess!

We are much more likely to carry out our commitments when we have made ourselves accountable to someone else. Establishing accountability with others for our goals and our behavior can keep us on target and eliminate a great deal of procrastination and sloppy thinking.

Most developing management theory centers around the idea of mutual sharing in the setting of objectives and a continuing dialogue between the "management" and those responsible for task accomplishment. "Management by

Objective" (MBO) assumes such a mutual accountability. It is useful in both salaried and volunteer organizations.

There is a great deal of pleasure in being held accountable. It is good to share our "victories" with others, particularly when we have been a part of the goal-setting process from the beginning. Yet at the same time, there is a certain amount of fear. The joy of success can turn to ashes in the day of failure. But success is only possible if the possibility of failure exists.

There are three kinds of accountability. The first is built-in to the situation into which we are born. If we expect to be a part of our society, we accept the accountability which that society places upon us. We are expected to do certain things correctly and according to schedule. Taxes will be due every April. Stop lights will turn red. Such laws are powerful incentives to good "performance" on our part.

The second kind of accountability is that which we accept from others. When we join a company or a club or any human association, in essence we agree to play according to the rules. This may include taking instructions from "superiors," acting according to others' agendas and schedules. There may be a sharing in the setting of the goals and the schedule, but nevertheless, we are bound to perform most of the time if we want to remain in good standing with our group.

The third kind of accountability is that which we voluntarily make to others. We all seem to perform better against the goals we have set for ourselves and to which we have voluntarily committed ourselves than we do to the second kind (See GOOD GOALS AND BAD GOALS).

This third kind of accountability can work in a number of ways. At the organizational level it works when the superior not only invites his subordinates to share in the setting of their goals (telling him what he should hold them accountable for), but when the superior in turn sticks his neck out and invites his subordinates to hold *him* accountable for his goals.

In a fellowship, such as a group in a local church, accountability works well when each individual in the group makes an open commitment to the group for his own performance. I have been a part of a number of such groups in which the commitment level was really great. The sense of responsibility and desire to support the group by performing against such a commitment is extremely high. Mundane committees can be turned into powerful forces for forward movement when the group demands and receives such high accountability. The communists have exploited this dedication to the cell group to great advantage. It's a basic human (and Christian!) principle that works.

Accountability groups organized around common interests or problems are used more and more. Have you heard of the Presidents' Clubs being formed around the United States? Each member pays a high fee (as much as $1000) to join the "club." Each man must be the president of an organization. The rules of the club specify that at each meeting one or more people will present a problem. The others will then work out a solution with him. The individual then makes a commitment to the group to go back and test their solution and report at the next meeting as to how effective it was. Professional and non-professional accountability groups of this type can really help us keep our goals straight. (Even without a $1000 membership fee!) Weight Watchers and Alcoholics Anonymous work on a similar principle. (Many of us need to form time-watchers groups!)

At the one-to-one person-to-person level we should seek to be accountable to someone for as many areas of our lives as possible (and to permit others to ask us to hold them accountable). I have one friend who has often asked me the simple question, "What can I pray about for you this week?" I soon learned that he intended to accept responsibility not only to pray about my need, but to ask me a week later "How did it go?" I quickly discovered not to be too glib with my prayer requests. . . .

In the area of family living there are many built-in accountability levels, but it is important that we not only hold our children accountable for their actions, but that we permit them to hold us accountable to them (see FAMILY). This is where accountability really begins.

ALERTNESS

How easy it is to become so involved in a routine or so preoccupied with the task at hand that a good opportunity passes us by. Have you ever sat in a meeting and suddenly realized you really hadn't heard what the speaker had been talking about for the past four minutes? Have you caught yourself daydreaming when you really should be listening intently to what someone has been sharing with you? Have you ever wondered why some people in meetings object to issues that have never been raised? Most of the time it's because we have not been alert to what's going on. We have allowed our minds to wander off into some other area.

Staying alert is hard work, and I suspect that the person who is alert *all the time* would have difficulty living with himself. There are times when we just *have* to pull the curtain down against the outside world and turn inward for a brief while. But what about those times when you *want* to stay alert? How can you save time in these areas?

One good technique is to make the assumption that you do *not* understand what you are hearing or what you are seeing. Use this as an excuse to keep checking out by asking questions, repeating back what you have heard or explaining to yourself what you are seeing. (See LISTEN)

A second is to change routines. (See HABITS) Some routines are excellent, but others need to be continually varied because they become *so* routine we fail to use them. For example, if you use a things-to-do list regularly, you may discover after awhile you are ignoring your own list. Find another way to remind yourself of the same thing.

Tackle some new reading material on a subject that you have never dipped into before. Force yourself to understand the author's terms.

Continually look at each new individual you encounter as a God-given opportunity to relate to another person and to understand him and, therefore, all men in a new way. (See LISTEN)

Keep moving. Don't get too settled in that chair at work. Get up from time to time. Switch to a stand-up desk or another chair. Moving out from behind your desk to another chair not only gives you a change of position, but it makes your visitor feel you are much more open to him.

ALTERNATE PLANS

More time is wasted because no thought is given to alternate plans.

In doing your planning, think not of only what you're going to do if you succeed, but what you're going to do if things go wrong. If there's a possibility something can go wrong, it probably will (see FAILURE).

Plans are always revisable. Don't pursue them doggedly to the bitter end. Go on to "Plan B"! This will save you both time wasted in procrastination and time wasted doing the wrong thing. We are not talking here about double-mindedness being tossed hither and yon by this idea or that. Quite the opposite. When you are prevented from moving in one direction, make sure you have another way to go.

Have a regular review time alone to review your plans and your progress to see if your plans should be changed.

HOW DO I SPEND MY TIME?

An Inventory and Planning Sheet

Do you sometimes wonder "where the time went"? Do you have an uneasy feeling that you may be throwing your life away in little pieces? Do you see any relationship between the way you spend your time and the goals you have set for your life?

The first step to getting control of our time is to see where it goes. The second step is to make some deliberate attempts to plan our expenditures of time so that they take into account all the things we should be doing (or being!)

The enclosed form is designed to help you do both.

Taking an Inventory

For one week fill in for each day something you have done in each fifteen or thirty minute segment of the day. You will notice that the times on the lefthand columns have purposely been left blank for you to fill in, so you can include all your waking hours. People have different lifestyles that demand different allocations. If you get up at four a.m., start your day there. If you go to bed at 10 o'clock, end your day there.

It is helpful if you get someone to assist you in this. A wife or a secretary is a real help. See the sample on the back page.

Before you begin, make a list of your goals for the week in the left-hand side of the page. This should include not only job and task-oriented goals, but things you want to do by yourself, with your family, or with others.

At the end of the week, review your time spent against the goals. How much did you spend on each one? How many did you accomplish?

Planning a "Standard Week"

A second way to see this form is to think through your week in terms of those things which tend to repeat themselves each week—meetings you have, regular appointments (meals with your family!), as well as blocks of time you have set aside for special kinds of tasks. See the three samples on the back page. "Standard weeks" are useful in that they let you fill in all the non-standard things in the holes that are left, and they help you visualize how you are spending your time.

Planning Ahead

Whether or not you have a standard week, the form on the inside is a useful desk-size calendar to keep track of all your plans for the coming week.

World Vision International 5/73

WEEK BEGINNING:		SUNDAY	MONDAY	TUESDAY
	:00		Awake + dressed	
Goals for this Week:	:30		Breakfast with family	
1._____	:00		Read together / Drive to office	
2._____	:30		Look over mail	
3._____	:00		Sorted for reply / Worked on sermon	
4._____	:30		Got notes together / Read	
5._____	:00			
6._____	:30		Made sermon outline	
7._____	:00		Talked to Secretary / Phoned Joe Bailey	
8._____	:30		Called 13 people / Talked 12 people	
9._____	:00		Drove to Birmingham / Lunch with Jim	
10._____	:30			
	:00			
	:30		Drove back to office	
	:00		Counselled Mr. M.	
	:30			
	:00		Counselled Mr. J.	
	:30		Phone calls / Visited at hospital	
	:00		Saw Mrs. R.	
	:30		Talked to Dr. Jacks / Did dictation	
	:00		Drove home / Read Newspaper	
	:30			
	:00		Had dinner	
	:30		Read Newspaper	
	:00		Drove to Meeting / Board Mtg.	
	:30			
	:00			
	:30			
	:00			
	:30		Drove Home / Talked to wife	
	:00		Went to sleep	
	:30			
	:00			
	:30			
	:00			
	:30			

	WEDNESDAY	THURSDAY	FRIDAY	SATURDAY
:00				
:30				
:00				
:30				
:00				
:30				
:00				
:30				
:00				
:30				
:00				
:30				
:00				
:30				
:00				
:30				
:00				
:30				
:00				
:30				
:00				
:30				
:00				
:30				
:00				
:30				
:00				
:30				
:00				
:30				
:00				
:30				
:00				
:30				
:00				
:30				

ANALYZING YOUR TIME

The first step to effective time management is to analyze the way you are presently spending your time. Time is life! Analyzing how you spend your time is analyzing how you spend your life — all of it! There are two ways of doing this. The first is to compare your time investment with the goals you have set for yourself — all of them — and then discover things to be added or subtracted. The second is to analyze your time by categories or types of things you are doing. Where are you using your time? Could you be more effective?

Analyzing your time against your goals. First, write down each one of your personal goals. Make sure it really is a goal (see GOALS). Give each one of your goals an identifying number for easy reference.

Second, make a list of all tasks which require your time and all the people (including yourself) with whom you are presently spending time. This will give you some idea of your present commitments to yourself and to others. Write down next to each one of these commitments the number of the goal (if any!) involved.

Third, for one week keep track of everything you do in thirty minute increments (see INVENTORY and *"How Do I Spend My Time?"* p. 21). Note against each block of time the goal for which this time was spent.

Last, take a look at your monthly calendar and your weekly or daily calendar (or whatever system you use to plan your life), and note for each one of your appointments which one of your goals was met by this appointment.

This can be an alarming and disturbing exercise. You'll probably discover there are large blocks of time which are not related to your goals *as you now perceive them.* Consider if they are related to any goals, and if so which ones. Don't be discouraged too quickly. If 50 percent of your time (not counting your sleep time) was spent on your goals, you're probably doing marvelously well. (But see LIFESTYLE)

Categorizing Into Groups. If it's not your style to compare your weekly time analysis and your calendars and your commitments against your goals, another way to get at it is to break down how you're spending your time into categories, either on an hourly or percentage basis.

These categories might have to do with *people relationships;* time spent with friends, family, work associates, yourself, etc.

They might have to do with *types of assignments:* professional, home, volunteer, etc.

They might have to do with types of work: physical, mental, emotional, etc.

Another way of breaking down time for those who are in management situations is to estimate how much time is spent in planning and innovation, control, organizing, staffing, directing, and specialist or technical work.

Regardless of which way you went at it, ask yourself *why* you did the things you did — why did you do some things you *didn't* want to do? In some cases you will discover that someone asked you to do it. In other cases you may have been interrupted and trapped into doing it. (See INTERRUPTIONS) Maybe there was an unexpected change in plans, or perhaps you've forgotten the original reason.

Analyze which of these were just time wasters. (See TIME WASTERS) What can you do about them? Which could you have delegated? Again, it's a matter of lifestyle.

Once you have a picture of where you are, set about making some new plans to clean up some of the time wasters, and concentrate on the most important things. (See GOALS, PRIORITIES, PLANNING)

Remember this is a continuous process. You keep changing. Times keep changing. New situations arise. You have to keep examining your goals and your values. How you're

spending your time is a reflection of their relative priority for you. Are you satisfied with what you see?

ASK

Before you start trying to solve a problem by yourself or design a new procedure, spend some time finding out if someone else has already done it. *Ask*. It will save an awful lot of your time and a great deal of that of others.

My first professional job was with a large aerospace company — 25,000 employees under the same roof. Three thousand of those employees were engineers. During one of my first mornings at work my group leader took me aside and made some suggestions on how to get the most things done in the least amount of time: "There are 3,000 engineers in this building. Most of them have more experience than you do. Keep asking questions."

Are you one of those people who is either too busy or too proud to ask? Whether it be stopping at the gas station to ask the way to an unfamiliar city, or seeking out some more experienced person or organization, asking pays high dividends. Three letters of inquiries or two phone calls may save endless hours and energy.

Before you tackle the next problem by yourself *ask* yourself:
- Who is more likely to know more about this subject than I?
- Who else is likely to have faced the same problem or gone through the same experience?
- Who is likely to know someone who knows how to do this?
- Is there someone else who has the same goal I have here, and therefore is likely to be solving the problem at the same time?

And when you call or write these people or look up

their references make sure you ask them do *they* know? (see EXPERIENCE)

But remember *you* are the final decision maker. Build on the experience of others. If you can, avoid their mistakes. Then move ahead on your own.

ASSUMPTIONS

We all have basic assumptions about life. These may be stated or unstated. These assumptions eventually work together to make up what some people would call a "value system."

Understanding our basic assumptions about life is primary to managing our *life*time. For the Christian there are some basic assumptions which need to be stated before we get on with the business of managing our time and managing our lives.

Assumption number 1: Because God exists, and because He stands outside of His creation, there is purpose and meaning to life.

Assumption number 2: Because there is purpose and meaning to life, it *does* make a difference how I act and what I do.

Assumption number 3: Life is basically relationships, and what is most important is how I act toward and respond to other human beings.

Assumption number 4: The basic Christian priorities are first, commitment to God; second, commitment to the Body of Christ, His Church; third, commitment to the work of Christ. The "work" must never take precedence over the Body. (see PRIORITIES)

Assumption number 5: God has a plan or a strategy for each individual and each group of individuals. Part of the Christian's task individually and corporately is to attempt to understand this plan or strategy and become a part of it, to be conformed to the image of Christ.

Assumption number 6: We live in the creative tension of the paradox of God's sovereignty. God is in complete control of His universe, and yet at the same time we have freedom to act and are responsible for our actions. There is no human or intellectual solution to that paradox. Living with it is what *faith* is all about.

If these assumptions are affirmed, they in turn will have a tremendous impact on our goals. Since effective management of our time centers around clear and God-honoring goals, these assumptions are the key to good time management.

Notice how liberating these assumptions are. The knowledge that there is meaning and purpose to life means I *can* make a difference. With my goals set, the way I manage my life to achieve them *will* have a part in changing the world.

I must understand that I live in continual relationship to others. It is only as I am part of them, and they part of me, that I am really alive. Realizing this keeps my priorities straight. God will get this work done. He is *pleased* with me when I consider people before "work"!

Expecting God to have a plan for my life, for my group, for my world frees me to leave the responsibility to Him and do my best to play my part in the great drama He is working out. "All things work together for good . . ." takes on new meaning.

And I don't *have* to understand the whole thing. However dim may be the mirror into which I look, I have adequate data on which to live each day. In the midst of hurt and tragedy and defeat, I have tested out the paradox and found that a life lived according to these seemingly paradoxical rules *works!*

B

BECOMING

You *can* become more than you are. Let's get on with it!

I didn't read a formal book on psychology until sometime after I was out of engineering college. The first book I read was Freudian in outlook. It assured me that by the time a child was two years old, half his personality had been fixed, and by the time he was four his destiny was determined. What parents did during those vital years was all-important. At that point my youngest child was five, and I had really had it!

What a relief it was years later to read Gordon Allport and discover there were other psychologists who agreed with the Biblical concept that you can become more than you are. What a joy it is to approach the future expectantly, knowing you have the capability to change it and to become a different person. Finding meaning in successes and failures, setting new goals, rearranging our priorities, laying new plans for the future — are all tools which have been given to us to spend our time (and our lives) in more meaningful and fulfilling ways.

BOSSES

Whether we call them bosses, superiors, co-laborers, or leaders, those friends who have been given charge over us have a way of taking up a great deal of our time. This can be a frustration or a reward. It can make us more effective or more ineffective. How do we make the most out of "boss time"?

There are probably people who would take exception at this point, but in my opinion each one of us should see making a success out of his boss as one of his primary goals.

Trying to figure how to make a success out of your boss is a great time saver. In the first place it reduces the potential conflict that may exist between your perception of what the organization wants and what your boss wants. It's my opinion that when this question arises you should always come out on the side of your boss (or change your boss!). The whole concept of superior-subordinate relationships in an organization is that the superior has a higher responsibility. If we permit *our* perception of what would be good for the organization to take precedence over what the boss has asked us to do, we will create nothing but frustration in ourselves and others.

In the long run, making the boss look good ultimately makes us look good. By "making the boss look good" we don't mean condescending with scraping acquiescense to every whim or suggestion. What we're talking about here is the priority of time — deciding which things come first.

How do you make a success out of your boss?

Learn as much about him as you can. What is his style? Is he a directive or a non-directive leader? Is he primarily a decision-maker or a problem-solver? What are his basic needs? How can you meet them! What are his weaknesses? How can you match them with strengths? What are his strengths? How can you enhance their value! To learn these things we have to keep experimenting and testing. How does he perform in meetings? What kind of memos does he write? What type of duties does he like to delegate?

Do things his way. This may not always be possible. My way and his way may be quite different, and yet wherever possible I should attempt to respond to his assigned tasks in a way which will be perceived by him as meeting his needs.

Represent him fairly. Every man has his weaknesses. There is a chink in everyone's armor. The longer you work for an individual the easier it is to identify these weaknesses. Work to strengthen his areas of weaknesses, but *talk* about his *strengths*.

Trust him completely! Trust is the essential glue of all relationships, without it, forget being a team! Here is the vital test: can you accept his actions without serious reservations as what you would do under similar circumstances, if you knew (which you may not), if you were subject to the demands he is (which you are not), and if you were uniquely he (which you can never be)? How does this help *you* manage *your* time?

When I start guessing what is best for the organization, rather than learning what is best from the one whose job it is to know, I am immediately taking responsibilities that are not mine. And that is no way to save time.

Any time I stop trusting him, I should bow out of the relationship. And that is a fine way to stop wasting your time.

BUSYWORK

Some people make real work out of keeping busy. Parkinson's famous law that the amount of work will always expand to fill the time available to do it has a great deal of truth in it. At times keeping busy on trivia can give us a false feeling of accomplishment. We see piles of paper flowing over our desks or numerous appointments being made, and we are lulled into a false security of believing that things are being accomplished.

Remember it is not how much we are doing that is important but how much we get done. A full briefcase lugged home every night (and sometimes lugged back in the same condition) is not the mark of an important man, but the badge of poor time management.

C

CALENDARS

In our modern interdependent society the only way we can effectively live together is to plan to act together and move together. Unless you are blessed with an unusual memory, the only way to keep track of these future commitments to one another (and to ourselves!) is by writing them down. A calendar is a powerful tool indeed.

Some people have not discovered the value of keeping *different kinds* of appointment and schedule calendars. There is great advantage in being able to picture at a glance the unit of time under consideration. Having a one-page yearly calendar, a one-page monthly calendar, a one-page weekly calendar, a one-page daily calendar is extremely useful for this purpose.

Yearly appointment calendars are available. Keep one on your wall. Use it to indicate such things as periods you will be out of town or blocks of time you have committed to other uses. They are useful for showing you your future commitments at a glance and for keeping the load you are carrying in proper perspective. (see RELIEF VALVES)

33

Monthly calendars of the type many people keep on their desks find their main use in noting items which fall outside of our regular routines (see STANDARD DAYS, WEEKS, AND MONTHS). They have the advantage of alerting us to what lies ahead, things for which perhaps we must prepare now. Monthly calendars are also available in pocket size and are handy for both the housewife and the executive.

Weekly calendars are used mostly for desktop work to control the daily and weekly routine, but they are also available in appointment book form. They give you the kind of space you need to control the details of your day.

Daily calendars, usually in the form of appointment books, are extremely useful for some people. Those which also provide a place to write down a "things to do" list and which provide a place for a diary and keeping track of expenses are particularly useful for busy executives (and busy housewives!)

Each of these calendars has its advantages and disadvantages depending on your needs and lifestyle. That is why most people find it effective to use two or more. The daily calendar gives you plenty of room to write down all the details of the day, but it doesn't help you to plan ahead. At the other extreme, the yearly calendar gives you plenty of plan-ahead information, but the amount of space in which to write all the things you want to do tomorrow is necessarily limited.

Calendars need to be filled up! One way of not getting yourself over-committed, or committed to things which have nothing to do with your goals, is to fill your calendar up with things that have to do with your goals (see FILL UP THE CALENDAR!).

And then Parkinson's famous law can operate in a favorable mode.

Remember that calendars should reflect a chain of events:

1) We set or check on our goals.
2) We make plans to accomplish those goals.
3) We schedule future events we believe will help accomplish our plans.

Therefore our calendars — our scheduling of *time* — most clearly reflects our goals.

CHANGE

In recent years we have been bombarded by an ever growing range of literature pointing out the fact that we are undergoing times of tremendous change. "Future shock" is getting to be an everyday phenomenon in most of our lives. Since each one of us is part of a larger group, and ultimately part of the world's system, we are caught up in the continuing flux of change.

It is here the familiar quotation, "Lord, help me to change what I can, accept what I can't, and be wise enough to know the difference," sums it all up.

When setting goals recognize that circumstances will change and goals will have to be reset for the future. Goal setting is a process!

When establishing priorities realize that what has a high priority today may have a lower priority tomorrow. Priority setting is a process.

When making plans recognize we are attempting to predict the future, and the future has a way of being unpredictable (see ALTERNATE PLANS). Planning is a process!

If we are continually faced with new situations, we may have difficulty adjusting to a rapid rate of change. The temporary employment agency places people in new situations continuously. For many it is a challenge. For others it is a real stress on their life systems.

Experiments show that people who are exposed to a great deal of change (new country, new home, new job, death in family, wedding, etc.) actually become ill after a certain upper limit is reached. Culture shock, which could be the result of simply moving to a new neighborhood, is a form of this phenomenon.

Look for signs of too much change, and strive to spread them out or reduce the shock.

When managing time resources remember what we spend time on at the moment reflects what we value the most at that moment. Our use of time reflects our value priorities and communicates our goal-hierarchy, including the priority we place on the value of change.

CHECKLISTS

Checklists are one of the simplest and yet most effective ways of organizing work and measuring progress.

A checklist is nothing more than a chronologically arranged list of the things that need to be done to reach a goal. It does not attempt to describe *how* each step is to be accomplished, but rather what is to be done and in what sequence. Herein lies its power and simplicity. This in turn is a trigger to make sure we ·know how to do it and what to do.

Checklists can be quite formal, such as the ones which are designed for preflight check of an airliner. They can be extremely simple, such as a simple problem-solving checklist (see PROBLEM SOLVING).

Here are two sample checklists, one for home use and one for business.

VACATION CHECKLIST	NEEDED?	DATE
Money into checking account		
Things-to-take list completed		
Neighbors notified where we'll be		
Paper stopped		
Milk stopped		
Police notified		
Garage locked		
Mortgage payment in		
Travel reservation made		
Car serviced		
etc.		

MAILING CHECKLIST	NEEDED?	DATE
List of names compiled		
Letter written		
Inserts designed		
Envelopes ordered		
Paper order		
Printing order		
Envelopes inserted		
etc.		

Once a checklist has been created to solve a problem or reach a goal, it becomes a kind of "standard plan" or standard procedure for carrying out that task. It therefore becomes very useful the next time we want to accomplish the same task. We don't necessarily have to follow the same steps we followed before, but we have a list against which we can check to see that we have considered all of the things considered the last time the task was done. We can then add essentials not needed then. It is a way of passing along both history and experience, even as we add to, modify, or simplify the checklist for our future use.

Checklists become powerful communication tools when we use them to standardize a task. Once a person is trained in the desired procedures, the checklist provides a healthy bias toward uniformity in future performance. In emergencies it can be an aid to the uninitiated in avoiding gross errors.

By listing the names of responsible individuals and dates each item in the checklist is to be accomplished, we have an effective way of displaying progress to everyone involved. As we cross off each accomplished item on the checklist, we quickly identify task status and those responsible for continuing them.

Checklists can be constructed for almost any kind of a plan. After they have been used over and over they eventually become habits. (see HABITS) A good example of this is the housewife who arranges her shopping list in the sequence in which she knows she will find things on the supermarket aisles. After awhile she has memorized the supermarket so well that her mind will automatically remember those things she needs as she walks up and down the aisles. A similar habit-forming example would be the checklist procedure we use in teaching someone to drive a car. The standard steps to safe driving soon become habit as they are repeated over and over. The checklist there is an aid to recall when habits are questioned.

For ideas on how to quickly generate checklists see ORGANIZING IDEAS.

CLOSE DECISIONS

Avoiding decision making is one of the biggest time wasters around. In a good percentage of the cases *any* decision is better than none. To go to the left or the right or conscientiously stand still is better than standing at the intersection in indecision. A 50 percent batting average in making good decisions is a pretty excellent record (see MISTAKES). There are many people who may not be excellent problem solvers, but they're good decision-makers. They have the courage to analyze the facts quickly and make a decision, and then learn from and live with the results. Many times such decision-makers will out-perform the problem-solvers just because they keep things moving.

If, after you have clarified your goals and weighed all of the facts, it's a close decision between two routes, the chances are it doesn't make a great deal of difference what you decide. Just make sure you do! The result will prove a better teacher than further deliberation.

CLOSURE

Closure is a funny word. It obviously has to do with closing something. But it has more the sense of things moving to a conclusion. When we say we are "trying to obtain closure" we mean we are trying to bring things *together* in a way that will also conclude (this phase of) the task.

Striving for closure is different than just concluding things (see NO and KILL IT). It implies we are reaching the goal, and it's time to shut down the energy output in that direction. When there is enough evidence to show the job has been done well enough to meet the need, that's the time for closure.

Too often people don't know when the job is done or when there's nothing more *they* can do. (See PERFECTIONISM.) They continue to work or stew and wonder why nothing is happening.

How to get to closure? How to know when enough is enough? How to pull ourselves off the job and forget it?

The answers are as varied as our different life styles. If you are the kind of a person who tends to "over-design" or put more into a project than it really needs, schedule a reasonable block of time to do the job, but schedule it close to the due date so it is impossible to do more — you *have* to deliver. This works well on individual tasks for which you are totally responsible (writing a paper, preparing a speech or lesson). It is dangerous if you have to coordinate your results with the needs of others.

Another approach is to set up standards of completion for yourself and others.

Here the basic questions are:

— Does it meet the need?
— Is it practical, will it work?
— Is it ethically and morally okay?

If the answer to these questions is yes, shut it down, and go on to the next goal.

COMMITTEES

It is an interesting, if not exactly theological, statement that a camel is a horse designed by a committee. But there are probably also a few committee-designed horses that have turned out to be donkeys, and that may have been close enough.

One purpose of most committees is to share risks and legitimize decisions. Another purpose is information exchange and communication. A committee can be very effective as long as it has a clear goal or purpose around which it is working. The trouble is that most standing committees, e.g. church boards, continue to stand even after their goals or purposes have disappeared. Every committee ought to have as its first order of business some statement; such as, "This committee will self-destruct on such and such a date."

But how can we make committees more profitable and less time consuming?

Certainly *start with a clear purpose,* and make sure everyone understands it.

Select the right people on the committee, and make sure they understand why they were invited and what their task is.

Show progress as the committee moves along (see MEETINGS — FORMAL).

Make sure that neither you nor anyone else is serving on too many committees. There are some Professional Committee Goers who find great fulfillment in that role, but for most of us this is not an effective way to spend our lives.

It is important to recognize here that there is a big difference between committees made up of people who are working together regularly and those made up of people who seldom see each other. A committee formed within a particular department of an organization may be able to get down to business very quickly. They know each other's style and they have a general understanding of what each person is likely to contribute. They, therefore, accept arguments and statements much more at face value. On the other hand, a committee in a volunteer organization, such as a church, may have many members who are seeing each other for the first time. They need to spend time getting to know each other. The fellowship aspect of such a committee becomes very important, and time spent allowing each member to explain or expose himself to the others will pay big dividends in output from the committee.

COMMUNICATION

What a waste of time it is to be working hard on the wrong thing. Working on the wrong things is often the result of misunderstandings caused by poor communication. The more we learn about communication between individuals, the more we understand what a complex and difficult process it is. Each one of us brings to the communication process our own biases and preconceptions (see IF YOU ONLY UNDERSTOOD . . .) How often the truism "what you are speaks so loudly, I can't hear what you say" gets in the way of what we are trying to communicate! We communicate not only in person-to-person discussion, meetings, letters, and publications, but by lifestyle, environment, relationships, body language, and a host of other subconscious ways. What can we do to be more effective in our communication?

Learn what communication is all about. It's a two-way process. The giving of information is not communication. Communication only takes place when a message is formed in the mind of the receiver. He receives the information you transmit and then processes it through his past experience, the present situation that he is in, and his understanding as to *why* this information is being directed to him. What he "receives" is almost always different than what you "transmit." Read, study, analyze, go to school, learn what communication is all about.

Wherever possible, *design your communications ahead of time.* Use all the visual, tactile and even olfactory aids you can get. (see DIAGRAMMING) Decide ahead of time how *you are going to know* the information has been received.

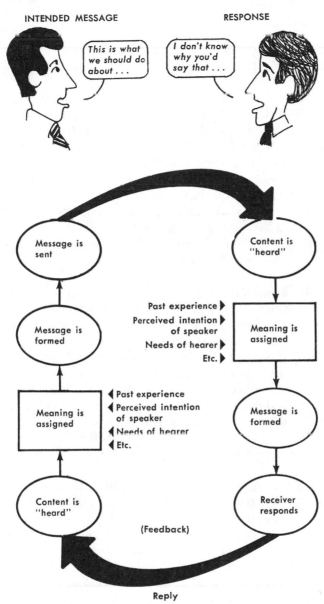

Get feedback in every way possible. Try to find out what other people are "hearing" you say. Help other people get feedback by repeating to them what you "hear" them say. Experience is a good teacher! Learn to "experience" others experiencing you as a communicator.

Learn to be clear and concise in your written communication. Understand the *purpose* of what you are writing. Attempt to understand the person whom you are addressing. What kind of letters is he used to reading? Will you need to restate a number of times from a number of different angles what it is you are trying to communicate? One of the basic rules of communications is: "First tell them what you're going to tell them. Second, tell them what you are telling them. Third, tell them what you told them. Fourth: take positive steps to find out what they heard you tell them!"

Establish regular information flow within your family and within the other organizations of which you're a part. This can be done by setting up information meetings (see MEETINGS — FORMAL), having a family council time, establishing organization publications, establishing reporting and check points. Set up regular sequences of operations and reinforcement of behavior indicative of "message understood." This is where the value of activity reports and progress reports give you feedback showing that what you agreed to is happening. Remember: many times failure to perform may just be failure to understand.

Choose the right method of communication. Some people respond better to the written word — others are listeners. Some people are really helped by diagrams and drawings — other people see things in terms of paragraphs and sentences. Do you really need a memo, or will a telephone call do? (See MEMOS) What can you do to make sure your main concentration is on communication that gets through rather than just getting it out of the way?

No one system will work. Use as many channels as the benefits justify cost. When it comes to communication don't worry about overlap, duplication or redundancy.

Sometimes you'll need as many channels as you can possibly find.

Assuming we have taken some steps to improve our own communciation, what are some of the things we can do for others to strengthen the communications process?

We need to see that *we all speak several different languages.* All of these are English! First we have our thinking language, which is our own personal language. It is what *I* mean when I talk to *me.* When we start speaking to others in this language, we often mislead them and communicate things that are quite meaningless.

Second, there is language of our personal group. This may be the language of our home, our office, or our profession. Sometimes it is "jargon." Christians in particular listen for "key words" to indicate the faith and belief of other people. Many times this "in language" covers up a wide range of differences which are not recognized by the group.

Third, there is technical language which is the jargon of science, trades, or the arts. This language is meaningful to those in the same field but becomes useless, many times counterproductive, when we use it with others who are not trained in this area.

Fourth, there is the language we share with society-at-large. The symbols the journalist and the novelist use, the words we use with people we do not know!

While most of us speak all these languages without any difficulty, blocks to communication come when other people use them on *us!* Many times we turn people off because we conclude they are being purposefully vague, or we see them as trying to impress us with their knowledge, or we come to the conclusion that whatever they are talking about is on the outside of our understanding. Or we think we understand the message, but it's not the message they sent! Communication stops at that point. (see LISTEN)

Edward T. Hall, *The Silent Language* (Doubleday Garden City, 1959) is a pioneer work that shows how much our culture affects our communication.

COPIES, BANE AND BLESSING

The low-cost, high-quality copying machine has made distribution of information extremely simple. It has also caused all kinds of problems for people who are getting too much information (and also a few problems with people who'd like to keep their material copyrighted!).

On the positive side, sending copies to everyone concerned is one way of keeping them informed, cutting down on the number of meetings, and giving people a sense that they're in the know. It's an excellent way of storing information in a number of different places and organizing material.

On the negative side, it fills up all kinds of filing space (see FILE DRAWERS), and it can cause all kinds of wasted time and useless reading.

Use copies of memos creatively. Try to avoid communcating the idea to people: if you don't get a copy, there's something wrong. And don't get trapped into filing copies of everything. Probably the best file for most items is the wastepaper basket.

Making copies of various quotes and other items of interest is a great way of rearranging ideas and sorting them out. Having to take ten books and note each page with a book mark and then refer back to them can be a big time consumer. Having copies of those pages arranged the way you want them not only saves time but enhances the creative process. I still remember the shock of going to a graduate school (seminary) at age 40 and having a professor hand me a bibliography of books for reference. I quickly learned I could build my own reference system by photocopying tables of contents and key sections.

CREATIVE TIME

There are some things we can do in small bursts, but when the time comes to dream large dreams, lay complex plans, paint a picture or write a book, it can't be done in small pieces. This kind of creative work takes large chunks of time.

If we recognize this, and our goals include such objectives, we will set aside such time and protect it. (see FILL UP YOUR CALENDAR) If your home or professional working environment is not one which permits you to have large blocks of uninterrupted time, then change the environment. (see ENVIRONMENT) Get out of the office or out of the house. Go to the public library or the local school library. Drive out to your favorite beach, mountain, or stream, or tear out the telephone and lock the door!

Try to identify environments and situations which seem to trigger your creativity. Consciously arrange to be in such situations when there is creative work to do.

But recognize that you need these blocks of time to work creatively.

CRISIS!

Crises come in all sizes. Big ones, little ones, middle size ones. Some people enjoy them. (see FIREFIGHTING) Some panic, some employ crises as a conscious leadership style. Other people just take crises in stride as part of their decision-making responsibility. (see DECISION MAKING)

When a crisis hits or is contrived for you, there are a few things helpful to remember:

Take time to plan. If you are informed that you only have ten minutes to make a decision, use five of those to do some planning. Results will almost always be better.

Turn a potential failure into a feature. (see FAILURE)

Use the crisis rather than let the crisis use you. Many times the very fact of the crisis is what is needed to mobilize people to action.

Reflect on the crisis experience later. We seem to learn more from wars than from peace, from conflicts than from consensus, from failures than from success. But don't forget to learn! You may be able to avert the next crisis!

D

DEADLY ENEMY

Planning for the future can be an exhilarating experience. It can also be a misleading one. Solutions to problems which look good on a bright Monday morning have a way of turning sour on Friday afternoon.

We need other people off whom we can bounce our ideas and share the enthusiasm of our projects. However, often our very enthusiasm keeps others from making either wise or considered evaluations. One way around this difficulty is to invite others (or yourself!) to become a Deadly Enemy of the plan or solution you propose. Let them attack it from every possible angle. Is it the most effective use of time? Does it meet the objective? Is the objective part of a large purpose? Is it the most effective way to go, considering cost? Can we afford it? Will it build or weaken relationships? Is it ethical? Is it biblical? What happens if it fails? What *unexpected* side effects will it have if it *succeeds?*

List all the difficulties quickly without attempting to solve all of them, so you will have as complete a picture as possible. (see ORGANIZING IDEAS) Then see whether your plan will stand up under the attack or needs to be modified.

A good variation of this is for you to take the role of the Deadly Enemy of your own plan and let others attempt to defend it.

DECISION MAKING

Every day of our life seems to be filled with decisions. Like crises, they come in all sizes. Large ones, small ones, important ones, trivial ones. When faced with too many decisions most of us begin to retreat to areas where the decisions are either fewer or appear to be less dangerous. Vacillating over a decision or worrying over whether we have made the right one takes both time and energy.

Most of us know the elements of good decision making processes:

Identify the problem and try to uncover the causes. Clearly stating the problem is usually 50 percent of the solution.

Determine the alternatives, including doing nothing.

Compare all the alternatives and select the one that appears to be the most appropriate.

In this way decision making is closely related to problem solving. (see PROBLEM SOLVING) However, in many instances there is just not enough time to go through this rather clinical approach to decision making. (see CLOSE DECISION)

Another problem of decision making is one of awareness. We may not be aware that there is a problem which needs ·a decision. Or we may not be aware of the alternatives. We may not be aware as to who should make the decision, or we may have no criteria on which to make the decision. Good decisions demand not only good experience (see EXPERIENCE), but they also assume we have the data to identify the problem. We don't need *all* the data. We only need enough data to make one which will satisfy those about us whose judgment is relevant in such

50

things. Satisfactory decisions, therefore, require a sensitivity to the values of others, a constant probing of the future and constant feedback of progress against plans. Most people think there is virtue in a fast decision. There usually isn't, although often there is a clear time when decision is needed. The more important it is, many times, the more reasons for delay. (see URGENT OR IMPORTANT?) Just be sure you make the decision, make it at the strategic time it is needed, and *know* you made it!

DELEGATION

Everyone knows that one way of saving time is to "Let George do it." The idea·that a good manager gets things done through others has been around for a long time, but most people are not very clear as to what they can and cannot delegate:
— You cannot delegate *your* job, because by definition it is your job. This implies that one needs a clear understanding of what his job is.
— You cannot delegate that which *only you can do* (by definition!)
But there are also some things you should delegate:
— You should delegate those things you *can't* do. Cut the expense of wasting time on something which you really don't know how to accomplish, even though it may be a blow to your ego.
— You should delegate those things which others can do *better* than you can do (if there is really someone available to delegate it to).
— Delegate those things you *shouldn't* be doing because they are not part of your primary goals or primary tasks.
All of this applies both to your business or professional situation as well as to your social and family situation. (see FAMILY)

How can you decide what is best to delegate? First, make a list of all the different types of things you are doing. Next to this put some columns headed MUST DO, CAN'T DO, SHOULDN'T DO (see A, B, C's). After this put a column labeled WHO CAN? Check each of the items on your list and see which of the things you're doing really should be done by someone else.

There are a number of pitfalls to delegation which should be avoided:

— Make sure the one to whom you're delegating *knows* he has the ball.

— Make sure your instructions are clear and the task is well defined.

— Make sure you are confident that the person to whom you delegate can do the job, or if you are not certain he can that you are willing to let him fail (see EXPERIENCE).

— Make sure you've given him all the needed authority as well as the responsibility (remember the responsibility is still *also* yours!)

— Try to put what is wanted in the form of a goal he can "own"! (see GOOD GOALS AND BAD GOALS)

It is important to realize delegation does not mean "go do it and don't bother me." Many times those receiving a job fail to recognize the limits of delegation that have been given to them. There are definite levels. Example:

1) Do it, and don't report back.
2) Do it, and let me know what you did.
3) Let me know what you intend to do, and go ahead and do it unless you hear from me.
4) Investigate all the available alternatives, and make a recommendation to me as to what should be done.
5) Give me all the information available, and I will make a decision.

There are many reasons people fail to delegate and therefore fail to manage their time effectively:

1) They don't have clear goals, procedures, or pol-

icies and therefore they have nothing to delegate. (see GOALS)

2) They don't understand how to check on the *subordinate* to whom they want to delegate. (see ACCOUNTABILITY AND FOLLOW-UP)
3) They lack confidence in their subordinates. (see PEOPLE)
4) They have a fear they will have nothing to do if they delegate this to someone else. (see BUSY WORK)
5) They believe they can do the job better and faster themselves.
6) They have failed to train their subordinates for major decisions. (see TRAINING)
7) They believe that unless the person is a subordinate, delegation is usually not considered an option.

There are also a number of reasons why we don't like to *accept* delegated responsibilities. Some of these might include:

1) We don't trust our boss. (see BOSS)
2) We are afraid of making mistakes. (see MISTAKES)
3) We don't know how to do the job.
4) We don't really understand what needs to be done. (see COMMUNICATIONS)
5) We don't see the reason for the delegation. (see GOALS)
6) Who does he think he is anyway, my boss?

In all of the above it should be remembered that delegation will not necessarily save the *total* amount of time involved, although the quality may improve. It is primarily aimed at saving *your* time. The economic principle of comparative advantage, of course, is that there are alternate things you and the person receiving the delegation could work on which will be of more benefit to you and/or your association or organization than the costs involved in the transfer.

One last point. Remember delegation is a two-way street. You have no more authority than your *subordinates* are willing to delegate *upward* to you. (Think about that awhile. . . .)

DIAGRAMMING

"A picture is worth a thousand words." Why not use one and save that thousand? Few of us are good artists, and if we had to paint a picture of something we had seen, most of us would be better off to try to explain it with words. And yet most of us *can* draw simple diagrams or charts which are highly communicative. A good example is the simple map you draw to show someone how to get to your home. It may be completely out of scale, and most of the bends and turns may be inaccurate. But it is much easier than trying to write it all out in sentences, and lots easier to follow.

Diagrams have a two-dimensional character that words cannot replace. They also have the ability to show relationships between a large number of different things or ideas.

One of the most powerful diagrams is the matrix, a few lines drawn like a tic-tac-toe puzzle, which show inter-relationships. For example, we might have a list of tasks down one side of the diagram and a list of responsible individuals across the top. The diagram quickly shows us which jobs are assigned to which people. Check lists done in this form are very useful. (see CHECK LISTS)

TASK	RESPONSIBLE							
	Joe	Pete	Bill	Jan	Lil	Ed	Ray	Di
Program	X		X					
Auditorium		X						
Ticket Sales				X	X			
Promotion				X		X		
Ushers							X	
Actors	X							X

Chinese characters are examples of a written language using only symbolic notation. There are limitations to such notations as a primary means of communication. Alphabetical languages, such as English, have much more flexibility. But they in turn are limited because they must be read word-by-word, line-by-line. One can only understand the complete meaning when he has read the majority of what is written. Any symbolic notation, once learned, helps pack into a small space a great deal of information. This is particularly true where a sequence of events is concerned. Thus to your question about the relative volume of my company's business over the past years, I may need two or three paragraphs to explain what I could easily explain graphically (symbolically) in a much smaller compass with much greater retention and understanding on your part:

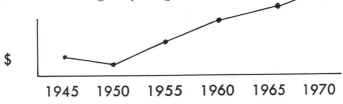

$

1945   1950   1955   1960   1965   1970

The preceding graph shows time relationships quite nicely.
I could also have shown it thus:

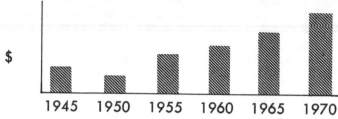

These graphs are familiar to most of us.
Symbols can be used to show relationship of events:

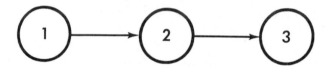

Here the event described by circle one relates to and
precedes the event in circle two which in turn relates to
and precedes event three.

Some of you will be familiar with the tennis tourna-
ment play-off diagram:

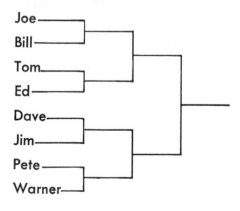

Joe will first play Bill. Tom will play Ed. Dave will play Jim, etc. The winner will move to the next location and play the winner of the adjacent pair. This diagram conveys quite an amount of information:

1. It shows who will play whom to start.
2. It shows how many opponents the winner must beat.
3. It shows possible advantages and disadvantages (Joe may be the better player than Bill, Tom, and Ed and still be a poor player who is badly beaten in the final).

Such a diagram has *logic.* It shows relationships. It has a great many uses in noting various possible combinations of events and forecasting their outcome.

One widely used logic diagramming technique is called PERT (Program Evaluation and Review Technique). Let's take a brief introductory look.

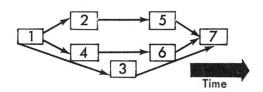

Time

This diagram also has to do with *events.*. Time moves from left to right. Events 2 and 4 are .dependent on event 1 but independent of each other, e.g. having decided to launch a new program in the church, I can talk to the staff and some members of the congregation at the same time. Having obtained a green light at 4 I can talk to two other groups independently (5 and 6), but I need both their approvals before I can draw up a final plan (7), and wisdom dictates that before launching the program, I have staff agreement (3). This is the *logic* of the situation. If you replace the numbers with names of individuals or groups in your organization, you will recognize you have gone through such logic yourself. Here the picture (symbols) says very quickly and clearly what words take time to convey.

These are just a few examples of using symbols to explain and communicate. There are many others, and the good time manager will take time to master the ones that help his situation best.

So far we have shown a few symbolic relationships that are "open ended." The first event relates to the last, but is not in turn affected by it. Other notations can be used to show such relationships:

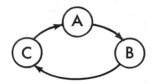

Here A affects B, B affects C, and C in turn affects A. In a social situation we may be describing a self-help project or the route of a rumor.

Or we might "say" it this way:

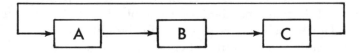

It says the same thing, except that the first picture showed rather a cyclic effect and the last diagram is sometimes described as showing "feedback," with a modification inferred. For example, a pastor may preach a sermon (A), which motivates people to give a Christian witness (B), bringing non-Christians into the church (C), and thus forcing the pastor to modify the content of his sermons (A).

Another useful symbolism that has profound meaning in American society is the organization chart:

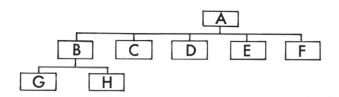

Again most of us understand that B, C, D, E, and F all report to A, while G and H report to B.

Such symbolic notation has more appeal to some than others. However, it is doubtful that any successful manager in a leading American organization does not use it in some form as a tool of the trade.

I recommend it to you.

DIVIDE AND CONQUER

Benjamin Franklin is quoted as having told the Continental Congress "If we don't hang together, we'll hang separately." He recognized that the easiest way to overcome opposition is one by one.

There's a basic principle at work here that can be used over and over. Almost any problem may seem too big for us to handle, but when we break it down into its parts it doesn't appear so formidable. (see PROBLEM SOLVING)

Projects and problems can be divided and conquered in a number of ways:

— *In time* we can break them down to each step needed to reach the goal, steps that are small enough to take. Take that first step.

— *Functionally* we can break them down by the dif-

59

ferent types of tasks to be done. Perhaps we can do one of those.

— *Strategically* we can break them down until we identify the person or one action that is the key to further unlocking the problem.
— *In terms of goals* we can break them down into subgoals and decide which are obtainable now. (see GOALS)
— *Geographically* we may divide them up so we can cover each part systematically.

Next time you are stopped in your tracks by a mountain of a problem, try dividing it up and conquering it, molehill by molehill. It works.

DON'T DO IT!

It is an American proverb: "Never put off until tomorrow what you can do today." The European approach is quite the opposite: "Postpone everything you can. You may not have to do it tomorrow!" (see PROVERBS)

There are two basic ways to save time. One is to do the things we should do more effectively or efficiently and in proper priority. (see A, B, C's) The second is not to do things we shouldn't be doing at all.

Make a list of all the things you are doing in your life right now. Examine your calendar. Check off each thing which you really *shouldn't* be doing.

Don't do it!

EASY THINGS FIRST

Many people need to get their minds in gear before they go to work. They need a little "practice" before they tackle the harder task.

If you are faced with the job of doing something that needs considerable creativity or one which requires a great deal of concentration, sometimes it's very helpful to get the easier tasks out of the way first.

If you're one of those people who needs to "warm up" at the beginning of the day's schedule, then do a block of small things and get those out of the way. The sense of accomplishment it gives you and the warm-up time provided will be useful for the larger task.

But doing the easy things first can be dangerous, if the hard things never get done. (see HARD THINGS FIRST! and BUSY WORK)

ENERGY

People have varying amounts of energy at varying times. Most women recognize they have periods of the blahs, but few men realize they have similar cycles which they go through on a regular basis.

Some people have more energy output in the morning, others have higher energy output in the afternoon. Some people are "day people." Some are "night people."

Recognize when your ups and your downs occur, when you have high amounts of energy available, and when you have low amounts. Use the high energy times for creative tasks and important problem-solving for which energy requirements are high. Use the times when your energy is low for simpler tasks like making phone calls, holding conferences, and doing short-cycle tasks. Design your day and week to take these energy patterns into account. (see STANDARD MONTHS, WEEKS & DAYS)

Also recognize these energy levels in others. You will discover some of your friends and associates have great difficulty staying awake at certain times of the day. Avoid calling meetings in which they are involved at times when you know they're not usually "with it."

Work at building up your energy. (see KNOW YOURSELF) Figure out how and when you operate best and work at exploiting your energy potentials. (see LIFESTYLE)

ENVIRONMENT

People have been arguing for years whether our heredity or our environment has the greatest impact upon us. The very fact that they are arguing indicates our surroundings and the situation in which we are operating certainly have a great deal to do with how we work. (see KNOW YOURSELF and LIFE STYLE) Most of us know one can't do much serious reading when his three-year-old is climbing on his lap and pulling his hair. Fewer of us recognize that many times our working environment is having the same effect upon us. We use up energy trying to overcome the background noise of the environment and waste a great deal of time with interruptions. Our work output is dependent first on us as individuals and then on our environment. In most cases it's much easier to change the environment.

So take a look at the "work space" where you are doing your job, or where others are doing theirs. Are all the tools available? Is the material you need reasonably close at hand? Are unneeded interruptions prevented?

Studies have shown that noise has a detrimental effect on work output. People in a noisy situation usually accomplish less than those in a quiet situation. See what you can do to put sound covers on constantly used electric typewriters or other noisy machines. Use sound deadening materials in your study or in your office.

If you can't correct the environment, then change it. Get out of the office to do creative work. (see CREATIVE TIME) This could apply to you individually and to a group. Many times a "retreat" situation is the most effective way to get a group to come to bear on its planning or problem-solving task.

If possible, use lunch times to create the better environment for what you want to accomplish. This can be done by either leaving the office to be alone, or if it is a "working" lunch, spending the extra money to find a quieter restaurant.

Remember your environment is speaking to others, and the way that you have arranged it communicates a great deal about you.

And remember too that environment is not just inanimate things. Environment includes relationships and feelings and understanding. One of our primary goals in an organization should be to create an "enabling environment," one in which those who are attempting to achieve a task have all of the material, social, and spiritual support they need to carry out that task in the most effective manner. If the task can be done better in a different organizational environment, it will pay big dividends to change the environment.

EXCELLENCE

Half the enjoyment of life is doing things *well*. How frustrating it is to have to settle for a half-done job!

Most of us recognize there are some things we'll never learn to do well, and it probably doesn't make any difference whether we do or not. But our primary goals — those which we feel called to accomplish during our lives — can be achieved with excellence.

There are some times in life when a person is put in a position of having to do a job because he is the only one available to do it. But if most of the time you don't feel you can do well what you are doing, it is probably best if you reexamine yourself and your job (see GIFTS) and switch over to doing those things you can do well. Life is too short to spend it half-heartedly. (see LIFE STYLE)

EXPERIENCE

The story is told of a crusty old bank president who was about to retire. The board of directors had passed over a number of older men and had chosen a fast-rising young executive as his replacement. One morning the young president-to-be made an appointment with his predecessor to seek some advice. "Mr. Adams," he said, "as you know, I lack a great deal of the qualifications you already have for this job. You have been very successful as president of this bank. I wondered if you would care to share with me some of the insights you have gained, those things which you believe have been the key to your success?"

Adams fixed him with his bushy-browed stare and replied, "Young man, two words: *good decisions!*"

"Thank you very much, sir. But how does one make good decisions?" replied the younger man.

"One word, young man: *experience!*"
"But how does one get experience?"
"Two words, young man: *bad decisions!*"
(see also FAILURE)

FAILURE

If "a miss is as good as a mile," then most of life is "failure." Seldom do we achieve 100 percent of what we set out to do.

God's standard of "be ye perfect as I am perfect" is a measurement against which one should continually examine his *progress*. As we try to make more effective use of our time, we should not be discouraged by failure to reach our goals. Rather, we should analyze the reasons for our failure, set new goals and move ahead. Personal goal setting is a process. We change, our needs change, others change.

Failure has a great deal to teach us as long as we don't fall into the "we tried it once and it didn't work" syndrome. (see EXPERIENCE) Practically every heading in this book could be a reason for a failure: failure to be accountable, failure to have alternate plans, wrong assumptions, poor communications, poor delegation, etc. The approach to solving the problem or achieving the goal may have been exactly right. Many times the answer to the question, "If you had to do it all over again would you take this approach?" should be answered with a resounding "Yes!" *(Only this time I would . . .)*

Many times failure can be turned into a feature. We may have failed in our employee relations program and lost a valuable employee. This is a great opportunity to reexamine our entire work force and do some shifting that could not otherwise be done. We may have to retrace our steps and do something over. This may be a good time to do something else we could not have otherwise afforded to do. People may be feeling remorseful or dispirited over a failure. This may be a good time to give them a more challenging or new assignment.

Failure is a valuable experience. Use it.

FAMILY

If managing your time is managing your life, and if our calendars reflect who and what we truly value, most of us would have to admit we're not doing a very good job with our families. This is especially true, of course, of the family "breadwinner," be that husband, wife, or both.

Few of us realize how complex are the interrelationships which exist within a family. The child born into a family in which there are already two other children faces a vastly different situation than that encountered by the first child. The total environment — physical, emotional, psychological, social, spiritual — within which each member of the family moves has a great deal to do with how effective each is as a person.

This makes it doubly important to keep our priorities straight. (see PRIORITIES) In a world which is continually changing and continually placing new demands upon us, it is important that we schedule and plan time for our spouses, our children, and our parents. Residual time is hardly the way to express the value to you of this most important and vital portion of the body and its divinely ordained relationship.

For those who may object that such a calculated setting

aside of time for the family seems mechanistic and cold, we can only respond that if a loving and free-flowing situation already exists, the addition of planned family time can do nothing more than enhance it. If, on the other hand, the family is not finding time for each member to build himself into the life of the other, it had better start planning that time, and the sooner the better! (see FILL UP THE CALENDAR!)

Family relationships are second to none in priority — except God!

To My Grown-Up Sons

My hands were busy through the day
I didn't have much time to play
The little games you asked me to
I didn't have much time for you.

I'd wash your clothes, I'd sew and cook
But when you'd bring your picture book
And ask me please to share your fun
I'd say, "A little later, son."

I'd tuck you in all safe at night
And hear your prayers, turn out the light
Then tiptoe softly to the door
I wish I'd stayed a minute more.

For life is short, the years rush past
A little boy grows up so fast
No longer is he at your side
His precious secrets to confide.

The picture books are put away
There are no more games to play
No goodnight kiss, no prayers to hear —
That all belongs to yesteryear.

For some insights into the flux of family life see Nathan Ackerman's *The Psychodynamics of Family Life* (Basic Books, New York, 1958).

My hands once busy now lie still
The days are long and hard to fill
I wish I might go back and do
The little things you asked me to.

— *Anonymous*

FILING

Finding things when you need them can take a lot of time.

The trouble with most filing systems is that they are designed to *store things* rather than *retrieve* them. Unfortunately there is no magic retrieval system that requires very little work to maintain.

In setting up a filing system first consider the cost of *not* having the things you want to store, and then consider how *quickly* you are going to have to retrieve information when you want it. Next consider *why* you are going to want it.

Some items can be stored under general categories for browsing purposes. Others are specific items, such as a copy of a letter, which are needed at a specific time.

A common practice is to file letters alphabetically by the name of the person or organization originating them. This has a number of difficulties associated with it. First, it forces one to set up a file folder for every individual with whom he corresponds. Second, if the letter is also part of a particular project, we must make a copy and file it also under some subject heading (and the exact subject is many times questionable). Third, most of us are notoriously inaccurate when it comes to filing alphabetically. Fourth, when we want a particular letter from an individual we have to pull the entire file folder to search through it.

A better practice is to file correspondence in the sequence in which it arrives. Each piece of correspondence is given a file number. The assignment of the file number is logged along with the name of the persons writing and receiving the letter and a brief of the subjects involved. The correspondence is filed by number. The same log number is also recorded on a series of 3 x 5 cards which carry on one the name and address of the individual from whom it came, and on others, the subjects it treats.

When the time comes to retrieve the specific document in question, if you recall who wrote it, a quick reference to the originator's file will quickly disclose file numbers in sequence by the date and subject, and the document wanted may be identified and easily pulled out of the file drawer. If you recall only the approximate time of its receipt, a search of the log listing of numbers assigned at the time will quickly identify the item by file number. Subject matter is also a means of file entry, if that is your basis of recall.

The advantages of this system are first that filing time is invested at the *storage* end rather than the retrieval end. Second, numerical filing is much more accurate than alphabetical filing. Third, much less file space is used. Fourth, the document may be recorded under as many different headings as are thought necessary for *retrieval*. Fifth, eventual disposal is facilitated. Sixth, if you file sequentially, microfilming of old documents becomes very practical because they can be photographed in sequence. The cost is minimal.

Good filing systems can be immensely valuable. Poor ones can be a pain in the neck.

FILE DRAWERS

If you have any, they're probably full. There's something about file drawers that just naturally attracts things people want to store. (see FILING) File drawers have a way of accumulating items that should have gone into the wastepaper basket. But the trouble is "we never know when we're going to need that piece of paper." One way out of this dilemma is to have a periodic time when you go through and have a Throw-It-Away Party. This is an excellent time to review past history and to recall ideas that were important some time back.

File drawers, like organizations, need to be continually pruned into oblivion so there's room for more useful and better things in the future.

If your files are arranged by date of receipt of correspondence rather than by the originator, pruning based on age becomes simple. After one year has elapsed, all one need do is quickly identify the 5 percent, that will ever be retrieved again and throw the rest away. This is easily done on the basis of subjects still of interest, today or in the future. This same principle of 5 percent can also be used to move records to less costly storage space, on the basis of age, if you lack the courage to throw it away. (see FILING)

And don't overlook microfilming. The cost is so low, it's cheaper than buying file drawers.

FILL UP THE CALENDAR!

A crammed calendar can be a blessing or a curse. If it's filled up with all of the things that other people want you to do, it can be an albatross around your neck. If, on the other hand, it's filled up with things which reflect your goals in life, it can be a tremendous defense against all the things that would intrude and detract us from what we want to do and be. (see GOALS AND PRIORITIES)

If we have our priorities straight, then our calendars will be filled with things in the following order:

1) *Time with God.* The times when you are consciously

open to Him through worship, prayer, meditation, or reading His Word.

2) *Time with your family.* The times when you are going to build into their lives and let them build into yours. Your calendar should show dates with your wife, dates with your kids, family time, time to talk, time to play. (see FAMILY) If you've never taken your teenage daughter to lunch you might be dumbfounded at her response to an invitation!

3) *Time for you!* Make a date with yourself! When are you going to have a relief valve from pressures? This means scheduling time for recreation such as golf or bowling, or maybe just time to do nothing — a time that is completely unplanned until the moment it comes. Look ahead at your monthly and yearly calendar and see what your load is going to be, and schedule in these times of relief. (see RELIEF VALVE)

4) *Time with the Body of Christ.* Times when you are going to be worshipping, praying, studying, fellowshipping together. This would include both time with the total local assembly, time for small groups (cell, church), time when you are going to be with other couples, and time when you are going to be in man-to-man or women-to-women situations. (see ACCOUNTABILITY)

5) *A time for other people. Unplanned* time when you're going to be available for *their* goals. This does not mean a kind of "professional" time for counseling, but rather the recognition that you are related to other people, and there are going to be times during your "work" day or during the rest of your day when others are going to need your help. (see PEOPLE)

6) *Time to plan.* Time when you're going to review your progress against your goals and make new plans for more effective performance. You ought to have a time to review each day, a time to review each week, a time to review each month, and a time to review each year. Using these times of review to share your calendar with your wife or husband and children can become a great communication device and an effective way of bringing your family together. (see PLANNING)

7) *Time for professional tasks,* plus all of the other things we do to live and earn a living (sleep, eat!).
You can use these commitments which you have made to yourself to explain to other people why the things they want you to do don't fit into your priorities. When someone asks you if you can come to a luncheon on Thursday, and your calendar shows you have a date with your teenage daughter, you can reply "I'm sorry, I already have a previous commitment." (Of course, you'll run into those people who will ask the question, "What is it you're doing?" This is the point where your commitment to your own goals will really meet the test!)

FIND OUT WHAT A GUY WANTS AND MAKE A DEAL WITH HIM

At first glance that seems like a crass statement. A Christian translation might be, "Discover a man's need, and help him meet it, and then he can help meet yours."
Almost everything we do and want to accomplish is in relationship with other people. The way to accomplish your goals is to work out ways to work in partnership with others. (see GOOD GOALS AND BAD GOALS) You'll never get far by concentrating on your goals at the expense of

those of other people. You may be "successful," but you'll also be an unrewarded person. What the other guy "wants" is a reflection of his perceived goals. If you can agree to help him with his, then you can expect him to help you with yours.

By the way, it's extremely important to both parties to understand what the deal is and how it's to be carried out in a Christian manner.

FIRE FIGHTING

People love to fight fires! Some managers manage by setting them!

It's a marvelous way of getting rid of all of your present responsibilities.

Some people are born fire setters and fighters. There's nothing they like better than the challenge of "Boy, we're really in trouble. This is going to require a full-blown effort!"

Fire fighting easily becomes a disease, and we soon become one of the indispensable fire fighters. (see IN-DISPENSABLE — YOU'RE NOT!)

If you find yourself or others fighting fires all the time, go light a new one entitled "Need to Plan." *A good solid day or week of fighting that fire may get rid of the rest of them.*

One of those fires just might get out of hand and burn the place down!

FOLLOW-UP

"People don't do what we expect. They do what we inspect." Sound rather totalitarian? There are some people who feel that "following up" on other people is not only manipulative, but downright non-Christian.

By follow-up we mean that some time after two or more people have agreed that something has to be done, someone takes it upon themselves to discover whether progress is being made toward the goal.

There are many good reasons for follow-up:

- We need to make sure the agreed-on goals still exist.
- We need to find out whether the instructions given were adequate and clear. Perhaps the person only assumed he understood the task, and he is proceeding in the wrong direction. (see DELEGATION)
- It may be the person has encountered problems which he either does not recognize or about which he is reticent to ask for help.
- It may be someone else is dependent upon this particular task, and they need to be assured the task has actually been accomplished so that they can begin theirs.
- It strengthens the relationship between individuals by demonstrating that one person thinks it's important enough to inquire as to what happened.
- It builds a feeling of accountability, one toward the other.
- It shows that the task is important. We are bombarded by so many demands on our time that we have a subconscious way of measuring the importance of the task by how much interest is shown in it by others.

There are many ways to follow up. The best way is to set dates along the way when follow-up will be done. Build in these check points during the initial planning, and be certain of agreement upon them among people with whom you are working. (see PROBLEM SOLVING) Display them so that everyone can see progress. Build in a reporting system so people can follow up on themselves. Know the people you work with well enough to understand what motivates them. Placing desired progress in such a "context of reinforcement" through follow-up will assure agreement on goals. (see ACCOUNTABILITY)

G

GIFTS

Know your gifts. Use that knowledge as part of your understanding of God's plans for your life. (see ASSUMPTIONS) Help others discover and develop their gifts so they too can live a life of meaning and purpose.

The Bible clearly states that each one of us has been given gifts (1 Corinthians 12:7). Sometimes it is difficult (and perhaps unnecessary) to differentiate between "natural" and "spiritual" gifts, but nevertheless we are assured they are there.

We need to understand what our gifts are and how to use them effectively. At the same time we need to come to terms with the fact that there are some gifts we don't have. (see KNOW YOURSELF) The Lord was just as pleased with the two-talent man as He was with the five-talent man (Matthew 25:23).

We also need to try to discover and to help others to discover what their gifts are so they can put them to work. An organization should be a favorable and enabling environment in which people can discover and use their gifts. This is particularly essential within volunteer organizations where "salary" is psychological. People become most effective when they are allowed to exercise their gifts for the good of the whole task.

GOALS

Everyone has them, though not everyone is able to state what they are! In one sense to have no goal is a goal in itself.

Managing your time has to begin with goals. How we use time must always be allotted and appraised in relation to goals, and if managing your time is managing your life, then the place to begin is with your *life goals.* The first step to good time management is to think through and write down what you want to be or do in your lifetime. When your biography is written, what would you like to find? Write down as many things as you can think of and then set them out in some priorities. (see A's, B's, C's) Now fantasize who you want to be and what you want to do and write down a list of things you would like to be doing five years from now. Check these out to see if they really fit into your lifetime goals. Allen Lakein suggests that we ask, "How would you like to spend the next five years?" Not how *will you* or *how should you* but how would you *like to?* (see PRAY YOUR PLANS) If one of your lifetime goals is to manage or lead a large enterprise, and you discover you would like to spend the next five years painting, there is an obvious discrepancy. We need to distinguish those things that others may have (perhaps falsely) taught us should be our goals from those which God has in mind and teaches us really to want for ourselves.

For a goal to be useful in time management, however, we have to know *when* we have reached it or accomplished it (or failed to!). A goal has to be *accomplishable* and *measurable*. When we say accomplishable we mean realistic, something which we have the faith to believe we can accomplish. When we say measurable, we mean specific as to *when* it will happen and how we will *know* that it did. Can we summarize it in terms of a past event? The goal "to have a large crowd at the Saturday evening meeting" is no goal at all. One man's multitude is another man's handful of people.

It's important to see that all goals are interconnected with other goals. Each event must take its place in the larger stream of things. If one of your purposes is to be an effective executive in your organization or an effective mother to your family, then there are certain steps which need to be taken to accomplish these things. (see DIVIDE AND CONQUER) These "steps" have become subgoals toward your higher goal or purpose. Expressed as "events," specific as to time and content, measurable and accomplishable, they may become the markers of the way to our life goals.

Goals must not be thought of as swords which dangle over our heads, nor need we be afraid to set goals for fear of failure. None of us can accurately know what the future holds, but images of what the future should and could be like are powerful motivations.

The Christian's goals are faith's response to God's imperative, and thus reflect an additional dimension, our part in God's plan. (see GOD'S PURPOSE/MAN'S PLANS)

Goals come in all kinds, types and sizes. It's useful to see that some goals have to do with what we want to *be,* and others have to do with what we want to *do.*

The *be* goals have to do with our attributes such as lovingness, kindness, righteousness, honesty, etc. They also have to do with our position, such as mother, businessman, worker. In one sense these goals are only measurable by our own standards. Objectively, they are measured by what we do about them. Therefore, they are worked out by *do goals.*

Do goals are the things we want to accomplish or the actions we want to take.

Our many personal goals can never be seen as separated from one another. Life must be viewed as a whole. One's goals for one's business, one's Christian service, one's family, one's friends must all be taken together. It is impossible to divide life (and time) up into neat packages. What life is all about is *people*, and people needs and people problems are all intertwined. (see PEOPLE)

Make a short list of your lifetime goals and another one of your year's goals. Put them on three-by-five cards and carry them with you. Regularly pull them out and review them. Can you account for your stewardship and time with your list before you? If you can't — revise the list, or revise your calendar!

GOD'S PURPOSE/MAN'S PLANS

The Christian continually experiences the tension of having to make plans for himself and at the same time trying to understand how he relates to God's purpose. It is difficult to maintain a healthy balance.

If we think it's all up to us, then we soon plan God out of our lives and therefore plan ourselves out of our relationship to Him.

If we assume it's all up to God, we deny all our obligations to Him.

God should be in all of our planning. All of our planning should attempt to reflect God's purpose as best we understand it. (see PRAY YOUR PLANS) "A man's mind plans his way, but the Lord directs his steps" (Prov. 16:9).

THE GOLDEN BALL — KEEP IT COVERED

Have you ever known this experience? You have a wonderful Bright Idea which you have worked over, polished and shaped until it is in the very best condition possible — a beautiful golden ball. You carefully (if figuratively) put it down in the middle of the conference table at your

---

For a programmed instruction differentiating between God's purpose and man's plan see the author's workbook *God's Purpose/Man's Plans*, available from MARC, 919 W. Huntington Drive, Monrovia, California at $2.00.

next meeting and sit back to bask in the oh's and ah's of others' appreciation? The response? Usually "very interesting. What's next on the agenda?"

Good ideas are like young plants. They need to be carefully tended and moved from one location to the next until they have matured. Transplanting them too soon or too late will not only waste time, but it may kill them.

Don't be quick to announce your good ideas. Take time to explore who will probably support them, and try to analyze reasons why others will oppose them. Hang onto your enthusiasm and divert it into building and communicating.

All good ideas have certain basic characteristics:

They are timely, being neither before or after their time. (see TIMING)

They are communicable. Others can understand them and build upon them (see COMMUNICATION)

They are energizing. Others can focus their own "golden balls" on them, or with reference to them.

They meet a need (see SOLUTIONS LOOKING FOR PROBLEMS)

An idea that meets these basic requirements is usually not isolated. It is a characteristic of good ideas that other people will be thinking about the idea at the same time. During the second World War Doppler radar was invented by three different companies working in complete independence of one another. Don't be surprised if you find others talking about the same things you're talking about, and don't assume they are reading what you are saying. You may be reading what they are saying, or you both may be responding to the same outside situation. Don't let that discourage you. Find out what your unique contribution can be, and go to work there. (see GIFTS)

GOOD GOALS AND BAD GOALS

To have some clear-cut goals is the very essense of effective time management. But goals are interrelated.

Sometimes our goals are not reached because they run contrary to other peoples' goals.

"Good goals are my goals, and bad goals are your goals," which is another way of saying two men cannot walk together unless they be agreed. If your goals include others, make sure when you set them that others "own" their part in them. "Good goals and bad goals" when properly handled can become "Our goals!"

The way to do this, of course, is to decide who else is part of your goals and share together in the stating of the purpose, the measurement, and the planning for the goals. For the Christian, this properly includes God. (see FIND OUT WHAT A GUY WANTS AND MAKE A DEAL WITH HIM).

As many people as possible should be brought in on the goal setting and planning phases of the project as early as possible. Failure to do this can have disastrous results.

HABITS

Habits are wonderful things. Most of us just could not get along without them. (Those of us who don't have any, are probably wasting a lot of time and energy trying to figure out what to do next!) So much effort has been expended on discussing bad habits that often we have forgotten to make a case for *good* habits. But good habits are a key to our effective use of time.

A habit is something which we do without thinking. It is something we have done so often it has become a part of us. It becomes a part of a total lifestyle. Driving a car is a habit. (Or it had better become one!) "Manners" are forms of habits which are acceptable and useful in social situations. Handwriting is a habit. The most useful habit in time management is a scheduling habit, one which automatically makes us think of where the situation we face fits into our total time frame.

But how do you get rid of bad habits or acquire good ones?

First, settle on a lifestyle, then identify what it is that you want to stop or begin with reference to it. See what forces are working to enforce the habit. Identify those which are working against it. Reinforce the former, extinguish the latter.

Next, seek for the triggers. Habits are often responses to situations. What is it that does or could cause the habitual behavior to occur?

Go through a problem-solving approach. (see PROBLEM SOLVING) Share your desire to change with someone else (see ACCOUNTABILITY), and then lay out a time schedule of reinforcement over which you will change your habits. Remember, anyone can break a habit or start a new one for one day. The trick is to keep habits of one day consistently following into another.

Every page of this book has its habitual aspects. Examples of good time management habits you might like to acquire:

1) Standard days, weeks, or months.
2) Problem-solving approaches.
3) Writing things-to-do lists.
4) Saying "no" more often when others' goals for you are not your own.
5) Replanning.
6) Write it down.
7) Checklists.
8) Listen.
9) Giving quality time to other people and yourself.

Examples of habits you might like to break:

1) Paper shuffling.
2) Procrastination.
3) Saying "yes" too often to the goals of others involving you, in which you have not participated.
4) Getting diverted by interruptions. (Sometimes we go looking for them!)
5) Not getting enough sleep.
6) Talking too much.
7) Working too much.
8) Perfectionism.

HARD THINGS FIRST

Procrastination is one of the greatest time robbers. One of the reasons for procrastination is that we are faced by a difficult task which we just don't *want* to do. Usually we don't want to do it because it requires some emotional involvement, some laying of ourselves on the line, the prospect of a point-of-no-return. There is that difficult telephone call we need to make, that sensitive letter we should write, that messy job we just don't want to tackle.

Do the hard thing first. Get rid of these emotional blocks through good life-planning procedures, and the rest of the day will go a lot easier.

But see EASY THINGS FIRST.

I

IF YOU ONLY UNDERSTOOD...

Each of us grows up with the idea that if everyone had the same facts we would all see things the same way. How many times have you said or heard someone else say, "If you only understood . . ."? By which they mean, "If you had all of the facts I have, then you would understand and see things *my* way."

But life is not like that. Each one of us comes to each discussion with years of varied experience, varied relationships, and varied environments, all of which modify how we "see things."

Once we recognize this tremendous difference in perception, we will save a lot of time wasted in imparting how we see the facts and find ways to identify what other people perceive the situation to be. (see LISTEN!) Then we can search for ways to communicate *through,* rather than around their perception. (see COMMUNICATION) Of course, we can never see things exactly the way another sees them either, but the event of experiencing others experiencing you, experiencing them in fellowship around the facts, can lead to better understanding.

INDISPENSABLE — YOU'RE NOT!

It is a humbling thing to discover that others *can* get along without us. (Which one of us has not harbored that secret thought that when we leave a job to others, it probably won't get done as well as it would if *we* were there?)

But the fact remains that none of us is indispensable. In the end, God's work *will* get done with us or without us.

The next time you get into the trap of thinking that job just won't get done without you, and you are about to commit another night to the office, ask yourself, "What will they do if I get sick, or what will happen if I die?" If you really believe you are indispensable, there's a good chance you've planned it that way — and all you have done is prove you are a poor planner, and no manager of time or talent of others.

On the other hand, there are *people* to whom you are indispensable — your husband, your wife, your children, your intimate friends. Your life is intricately interwoven with theirs. No one can replace you in this relationship. (see PRIORITIES)

But in relationship to a specific task you have been given to do or to manage, there's almost certain to be someone who can do parts of the job better (and probably faster) than you can. Admitting that fact can get rid of a big load of guilt and a lot of accompanying pressure. (see PERFECTIONISM)

INTERRUPTIONS

Interruptions come in two categories, welcomed and unwelcomed. Most of us are plagued by the latter. Sometimes, however, we fail to see that many interruptions are caused by ourselves rather than by others. We may be right in the middle of a project when we suddenly get a "bright idea" we just *have* to share with someone else. We leave our desk to talk it over with a colleague and ten minutes later when we return to the task, our train of thought has been hopelessly derailed, and the job is over. Sometimes we even interrupt ourselves verbally! Often I have found myself putting in a parenthesis during a conversation. I was just blocking my own communication by interrupting my own train of thought!

But outside interruptions are serious problems for most of us who are involved in tasks that require concentration. Before they can be minimized we must first discover the major causes. A good way to begin is with a weekly inventory. (see INVENTORY) This detailed accounting of our time should include not only when people stop by to see us, but also when we stop to get a cup of coffee or take some other kind of "break." Just recognizing a cause will often suggest a solution.

Many times we are interrupted by in-coming phone calls. (see PHONE CALLS — INCOMING) We should have given instructions to the secretary to hold the calls or perhaps taken the phone off the hook.

Interruptions can be minimized by scheduling set times when we meet with our associates, superiors, or subordinates. Probably the most effective way is to develop a standard day or standard week during which you expect and welcome interruptions from other people. This not only makes you more effective in your own work but gives you an openness which makes you more available to others to meet *their* goals. (see STANDARD DAYS, WEEKS, MONTHS)

Take a look at your office arrangements. The combination of an open-door policy and visibility to associates can be fatal to good "interruption" controls.

INVENTORY

Regularly we need to take a complete inventory of how we spend our time. Anything that will help us do this is a step in the right direction. But periodically, every six weeks, every three months, or at least twice a year, we should analyze a large block of our time (say two weeks) to see how we're actually spending it.

To do this make up a daily time chart in 15 to 30 minute increments starting from the time when you normally get up to the time when you normally go to bed (see pages 22, 23). Leave enough room so that you can make a notation of how you spent each of these periods. Make sure you note such things as coffee breaks, interruptions, driving to work, etc. You'll probably need help. If you have a secretary, ask her to do this. If you can, get your wife or husband to help. It sometimes helps to agree with a colleague that you will both do this and check up on one another.

It may be difficult to know ourselves, but at least we can know how we're spending our time, and how we spend our time is a good reflection of what we are.

This time inventory should be used to analyze how we are actually working in relationship to our short range and long range goals. (see ANALYZING YOUR TIME) Go over it with your secretary, wife, or colleague (or all three). If someone else has kept it for you, you probably won't believe the record. Use this inventory to establish new goals and rebuild your daily and weekly time commitments.

KILL IT!

Everyone knows there are only 24 hours in the day. Most people also seem willing to recognize there is some upper limit on what they or their organization can accomplish in a given period of time. How surprising it is then to find ourselves continually adding new work tasks without subtracting any!

Now new ideas are great. New opportunities are wonderful, and there are times when we ought to go ahead, even though we're not sure we can handle it. I once worked for a man who said the way to get ahead was to get yourself in trouble and fight your way out.

But for most of us this just won't work in the long run. So the first question we should ask ourselves when we are about to add a new task or a new involvement is, "What am I going to *stop* doing when I start this new task or take on this new responsibility?" This, of course, is a form of priority setting because it forces us to weigh new opportunities against the continuing importance of present ones.

There is a basic principle of renewal hidden in all of this. We are told that our body stays alive by some cells dying and new ones taking their place. Life involvements should be that way. There ought to be a yearly (if not monthly!) time when we're going to say, "What is it we're going to stop doing this year?"

This is not only applicable to individuals, but it's especially applicable to organizations. The organization that is not continually abandoning former ways of doing things, former processes, former goals, will soon find itself involved in doing nothing but keeping itself in business, which is another name for institutional maintenance.

Each year we should analyze the things we are doing and when we come to the one at the bottom of the list say, "Kill it." And the next — and the next — and the next — until we are back to 24 hours in the day!

KNOW YOURSELF

Learning to know yourself is not easy. One way, of course, is to know how you use your time. (see INVENTORY) But, to the best of our ability there is need to understand who we are and to learn to accept ourselves. (see LIFESTYLE)

Recognize that you have a number of roles to play. There are roles of leadership and roles of followership. There are roles of relationship such as father, husband or wife, or friend or sweetheart, professional/client, supervisor/subordinate. In addition to these major roles there are all kinds of other functional roles we are called upon to play each day. There's the role of automobile driver, the role of pedestrian, the role of supermarket shopper and many others you could name, all of which have their own set of rules and customs.

Different people have different energy levels and require different amounts of time to rest and think. (see

---

John Gardner popularized the idea of the need to eliminate outmoded involvements in his book *Self-Renewal* (Harper and Row). It makes excellent reading.

ENERGY) One man can't perform on less than eight hours sleep a night, while another manages (miraculously!) to get along on four. What one man finds emotionally draining another finds emotionally exhilarating.

All of us have energy cycles. There are times when we are much more creative than at others. There are times when our spirits are "up" and times when we are down. We need to identify these times and make use of them. (see ENERGY)

Some people absorb information by listening, others do much better by reading. What's your style?

Some people require a great deal of detailed thinking and planning before they act, other people move much more intuitively with seemingly the same results.

It is important to find out who *you* are, to know *your* style. Accept yourself and your gifts, and use them. God does! Have an overall style that reflects your goals.

Evaluate the pressures you're under and relieve them if needed. Tired people aren't effective people. (see KILL IT!)

Keep your priorities straight. Eliminate those things that don't relate to your goals. Feed your strengths and starve your weaknesses. Understand those things you do well and realize which tasks are best performed by others. (see DELEGATION)

You're the one person you are always going to have to work with. The more you know about yourself, the more effective you can become. And the more you can accept others for themselves, fine!

One way of getting to know yourself is through an analysis of ideal goals. On slips of paper write down some goals for what you would like to be or do, *if you had your* complete choice, ten years from now. Write down goals for yourself, for your family and for your work. (see GOALS) Now arrange them in order of importance. (see A, B, C's) These goals reflect your ideal self. You may or may not like what you see. You may discover there are some things you really wish were different. You may discover things you really should be doing that you are not.

KNOWING WHEN TO STOP

Some people don't have enough get-up-and-go. Other people just don't know when to quit. Quitting can have some great advantages. It really helps to know when to stop.

- Stop when you have enough ideas to reach the solution. (see PROBLEM SOLVING)
- Stop when you have done enough planning to reach the goal. (see PLANNING — HOW TO DO IT)
- Stop when the way you are doing things is obviously superseded by a better idea.
- Stop when you discover someone else is available who can do the job better than you can. (see DELEGATION)
- Stop when what you are doing is getting you nowhere. (see ALTERNATE PLANS)
- Stop when the time you have scheduled for the task has expired! (see ANALYZING YOUR TIME)
- Stop when sharing what you have done with others has more potential benefits in reaching the overall objective than continuing to perfect what you have. (see PERFECTIONISM)

Also see DON'T DO IT! and KILL IT!

L

LEARNING

The day we stop learning new things, we're in trouble. However, most of us find that learning takes more time than we seem to have available. This is probably because we have not clearly related learning to our goals. (see GOALS) But there are some things we can do to reduce the time it takes to learn all the things we should be learning.

Decide what you need to learn to accomplish your goals. Then figure out how you are going to get that learning experience, whether it be through formal training, association with others, or your own reading.

Find key publications that relate to your total life goals (see THE WHOLE MAN), and stick to these. Get rid of the rest. Don't read at random, there is no pot-of-gold at the end of that rainbow. One way of finding key publications is to discover what others in the field are reading, and what has been useful to them. Few publications are of complete interest to you. Learn to select from these what is most important and most unfamiliar. Look particularly for newsletters which are more and more available on specialized subjects. They cost more, but they're worth it.

Have a book reading plan that relates to your goals. Carefully select the ones you're going to read. Make them your own. Let them build into your life. Make sure the books you read cover your total life needs, including professional task, family, personal commitments, lifestyle, etc.

Develop different reading styles. A speed reading course can be very useful, but different publications require different styles. Learn how to scan, how to study, how to skip over those things which are not useful to you. Learn to pick out the unfamiliar for closer consideration, to pass over the familiar quickly.

Plan short learning experiences each year. These might be done with your family or with colleagues at your business. There are more and more short seminars and retreats which can really build into your life. (see TWO-TIMERS) Also make sure you've looked at what the local state college or junior college is offering in the way of night courses.

Learn from living. The laboratory of life has much to teach us, if we will only be willing to learn. Is your life 20 years of the same experiences repeated 20 times, or 20 years of progressive building into your life, and into the lives of others? See RESOURCES for ideas on different kinds of learning experiences.

LIFESTYLE

If you read all the advertisements in the magazines and on T.V., you might come away with the idea that there is one standard lifestyle for all red-blooded American men or women. There's the right car, the right clothes, the right food, the right house, the right job and a whole bunch of other "rights." The fact is that people are uniquely different and growing more so all the time.

Instead of adopting lifestyles which are more and more common, the Western lifestyles are becoming more and more diverse.

The first thing to do is to recognize this fact and not be appalled at your own divergence. (see KNOW YOURSELF)

The next thing to do is to try to make effective use of your own lifestyle and to make it work for you. If you have a lifestyle which fits into standard days, weeks, or months . . . fine, use them. If your lifestyle won't tolerate that kind of standardization, don't fight it, find some other way to work it.

Your lifestyle will be determined by a large number of different factors!
— Your personal values.
— Your commitments to your family, your friends and your job.
— Your physical and emotional makeup.
— Your education and experiences.
— Your natural and spiritual gifts.
— The environment in which you are living.
— The requirements of your professional employment.

The most important aspect here is to relate your lifestyle to your present situation. If it doesn't fit, come to terms with your concept of what your lifestyle should be — or where your life should be lived.

Don't forget to be accepting the lifestyle of others. . . .

It is interesting to see how inconsistent many of us are in our lifestyle. Too many of us may treat our children as adults but our subordinates as children. The young mechanical engineer may find himself some Saturday morning attempting to repair his washing machine without even thinking of what the "engineering approach" to the problem might be.

The point is that even though we play different roles in life at different times we ought to come to each one as the same person. There should be a unity of our goals and lifestyle which permits us to be completely authentic and "natural" in all we do.

Otherwise we will expend a great deal of thought, energy and *time* trying to remember "how to act" in *this* situation! And *that*!

LISTEN

More time is wasted by people talking when they should be listening. The trouble with too many of us is we start solving the problem before we discover what the problem is. (see PROBLEM SOLVING)

Whether it be your six-year-old boy, your wife or husband, your associate at the office, or your friend at church, every one wants to believe they have been heard and *understood*. Only then are they ready to fully apply solutions that others might have to their needs. (see SOLUTIONS LOOKING FOR PROBLEMS)

It takes practice to learn how to listen. It takes concentration. We need to look past what is being said to what the person is really trying to communicate. Remember most people speak at about 100 words per minute. Your hearing channels can actually absorb almost 400 words per minute, and your thinking process can probably function ten times faster than that. That leaves you large amounts of time to think what the person is speaking. How you fill in those times makes the crucial difference. Try to anticipate what the person is going to say. What are his intentions? What does he want to communicate? Keep checking out the facts and illustration you're hearing. Are they accurate? Are they biased? Are some facts (purposely) omitted? Mentally make an outline of the thoughts he's giving you. (see COMMUNICATION)

Watch the "body language" being communicated. Look for cues such as *when* the person came to talk, the circumstances surrounding the discussion. Repeat back what you are hearing in your own words to check out with the individual whether this is truly what he is saying. "Let me see if I understand what you're saying . . ." or "As I see it, you are saying . . . ."

In addition to practicing listening skills in interpersonal situations, set aside "listening" times when you are in meetings or working on problems. Think of listening as being the *input* time when all of the data for the problem at hand is going to be gathered. (see QUESTIONS)

Another great thing about listening is . . . we learn all kinds of things that way!

"Know this, my beloved bretheren. Let every man be quick to hear, and slow to speak, slow to anger" (James 1:19).

LITTLE THINGS (THAT BECOME BIG ONES)

"First things first" is a good motto. Getting rid of the top priority items before moving on to the lower priorities is a good way to manage time.

However, effective time managers recognize the little foxes that will nibble on the vines and eventually kill them. Little problems unattended have a way of becoming big ones.

Identify ahead of time these little details that need to be done. Schedule time during the day or the week to get rid of the details. Keep a running list of such problems or tasks. Plan ahead for the things you will need later on in the week, arrangements that need to be made ahead of time to accomplish a task or a trip, people you need to see to make appointments with, etc.

The cloud the size of a man's hand that appears on the horizon today may be a full-blown hurricane tomorrow.

MAIL — WHAT TO DO WITH IT

Reading and writing letters can be a time-consuming task. There are a number of steps to be taken to do this more effectively.

Learn to read faster. Use different reading techniques for different material: scan, speed-read, study, analyze.

If you have a secretary, have her underscore main points of letters and attach previous correspondence and other relevant material.

Have your secretary place important mail on top. This means you are going to have to train her to know what's important to you. Allot a set period of time for reading mail. In many cases it could mean you may never get to the bottom, and all of the "junk mail" will have to end up in the circular file.

Handle mail once. Don't shuffle paper! Take some action. That action might be to pass it on to someone else to answer in your name or to scribble some note that will bring it back to you at some future date for action at a

103

more appropriate time. Or it might mean it goes into the wastepaper basket. Just don't be guilty of sorting things into piles which then get sorted into piles and eventually end up in other piles.

Don't dictate to secretary. Use a recording machine. It may be nice to have a pleasant woman sitting across from you awaiting your every word, but it takes your time and hers.

Delegate your response to someone else by putting notes on a letter for someone's action.

Keep letters *short as possible.* You don't have to write eternally to be immortal. Do your debating, with yourself or the addressee, by more appropriate means of communication. Let your letters document agreements reached.

Handle by phone if possible, letters are expensive!: In 1972 the estimated cost of one page of correspondence (including labor) was $3.39. (see PHONE CALLS OUTGOING)

If you don't have a secretary, learn to type! Responding to mail by hand can be terribly time consuming. Consider using some of the multi-copy standard memo forms that offer enough space for a quick reply. This gives you copies of your correspondence and is a lot quicker than fooling around with carbon paper.

Throw away what you'll never read. Files are for "recalling" not "filing," so dispose of what you'll never "recall," retain only what you may, and dispose of that when your goals change (see FILING)

Develop *"standard replies"* for questions that arise repetitively. Put them on 5 x 7 cards. Code them and use them by code number in drafting replies.

Sometimes *write your reply right on the face of the letter* and send it back. If you wish a record of it, copy it!

Put interesting but not urgent literature in a "Trip Folder" to read on your next trip, or during your next session with the "boob tube." (see TV)

MEETINGS — FORMAL

Most of us spend more time in meetings than we think we should. Too much time spent in meetings is probably an indication of not enough work being done. But too many meetings are just poorly planned. They are the result of someone's "Let's get together and talk about it" approach rather than a planned part of a process of goal achievement. Meetings do have a unique role to play in accomplishing objectives. They are valuable in setting a "climate" for the task, in discussing information rapidly, in developing legitimacy for a given approach, and, when decisions are reached, in sharing responsibility no single individual could be expected to bear alone.

To have a "formal" meeting there are a few basic steps to take.

Have a goal for the meeting — both a long-range goal and a short-range goal. What is the *purpose* of this meeting? What is it you hope to accomplish? Could you get along without it?

Invite the right people. Who is really *needed* at the meeting? Avoid inviting people just because you don't want to hurt their feelings. Send them a copy of the minutes, take them out to lunch, or do whatever is needed to show them their absence is not an indication of disapproval.

Prepare an agenda with scheduled times on it. If possible, pass out the agenda ahead of time with a statement of purpose written across the top. Use it during the course of the meeting to manage the meeting toward its *purpose*, not toward completing the agenda as planned.

Provide enough time for the meeting. Make sure the decks are cleared so that needed time will really be available.

Be prepared yourself. If you are the leader of the meeting figure out who is going to need to be heard and what role you are going to play.

Start on time — regardless!

Make sure everyone understands the type of meeting you are having. There are three kinds of meetings:
— There are meetings to *announce* something already decided.
— There are meetings to *obtain consensus* for something which you have already agreed to do.
— There are meetings to *solve a problem* or *gather ideas* in which no preconceived solution is at hand.

A great deal of confusion and time wasting goes on when people don't understand what kind of a meeting they're in. A person who thinks he's in a problem-solving meeting when he's really in an announcement meeting can waste all kinds of time.

Take into account the needs of the participants in the meeting. Meetings of long-established groups and meetings of people put together ad hoc are quite different, primarily because in the former the participants have worked with each other and have been with each other over a long period of time, whereas in the latter the participants may know little of each other. (see COM-MITTEES) Early in the meeting build in the "getting to know you" process if it's needed.

Sum up near the end of the meeting so that it won't ramble to a close.

Announce the results at the end of the meeting, noting the action items for the next meeting, if such a note is needed.

End your meeting on time — regardless! A second meeting can be scheduled, and good time managers in the meeting have the next time period filled.

By the way, if you're invited to a meeting in which you are not needed, don't go! Tell the appropriate people your view and let them carry the ball. They will be impressed by your self-confidence and might just follow your example.

MEETINGS — INFORMAL OR PERSONAL

Hours of time can be wasted by people just "dropping in" when you are in the midst of another task. Sometimes the needs of the individuals must take priority over what you're doing, regardless. But a good deal of this informal chit-chat is not needed.

There are a number of things you can do to strengthen the informal meeting (see THREE-BY-FIVE CARD):

Avoid impromptu meetings by asking people to set up meetings ahead of time. Make sure you're able to respond to their needs. Make sure you have a time for them. (see FILL UP THE CALENDAR!)

Agree before you begin on how much time you need and when you will close, and make sure you have the time and that it's protected. If you sense the meeting will take more time than is now available, see if it is possible to schedule it for a future date.

Make up an informal agenda on a 3 x 5 card or a slip of paper ahead of time, trying to agree as to what decisions are going to be needed as a result of the meeting.

About ten minutes before the end of the scheduled time sum up what you have decided so far and ask your visitor to make his summation so you'll have time to make some decisions.

Close with a statement of what was decided and what action is needed next, and set a date for future meetings if they are needed.

Many people are much more effective in small one-to-one meetings, but they take a lot of time. Use them for problem solving and decision making, rather than information distribution.

Keep checking on yourself to see if the amount of time you are giving to different individuals is balanced. (see TIME FOR OTHERS) Don't let a few people absorb so much of your "for others" time that some people are shut out. A preferred procedure would be to include an appropriate amount of such time for individuals as a part of your planning, and see *them* if they fail to see *you*.

MEMOS

Early in my executive career I was a Memo Expert. When it came to pinning something (or someone!) down in writing, I could really do it. I had a well documented file on all the projects on which I was working, and had no difficulty at all in pointing the finger at the problem or person impeding progress.

It took me a number of years to discover (and I'm afraid I'm still learning) that memos and official letters can be blocks to communication rather than bridges. Too often we shoot from the hip and think later. Rather than a memo, make a phone call or a personal visit. Many times you'll discover the situation is quite different than it appeared at first glance.

There are times, of course, when memos can't be avoided, but whenever possible limit notes and letters to the following:

108

1) Commendation and thank you's (SEE THANK YOU)
2) A description of what has been already agreed to orally.
3) The transmission of information such as schedules, plans, etc.

When you have to write the "difficult" letter or memo, do your very best to put yourself in the chair of the person who's going to read it, and take all the time it needs to do a good job. (SEE COMMUNICATION) The more difficult it seems to you, the more time you should take in getting your facts together.

Memos are like arrows. They're shot into the air. They have a way of landing in places you know not where. Think before you shoot.

MISTAKES

The point is not whether we will make any — we will. (see FAILURE)

The point is to learn from them (see EXPERIENCE), and try not to make the same mistake again.

Decision involves risk, and in the making of decisions mistakes are bound to be made. Giving a person or a group an opportunity to take a risk (and therefore make mistakes), can be a rewarding experience if the stakes are not too high. If you or your organization are *afraid* of *mistakes* you will soon become paralyzed. If you make *no* mistakes you are operating too conservatively, missing opportunities, and are not likely to grow.

Admit your mistakes to both your superiors and your subordinates, and encourage them to do the same. If you are living in situations where mistakes are not acceptable, set about to change that environment or get out of it. To rephrase a phrase, "Nothing *fails* like success." Often little is learned from it. (see FAILURE)

N

NO!

How many useless things have you ended up doing because you didn't say "'No"? Most of the time we say yes because we can't think of any *reason* for not cooperating. The basic reasons for saying no should be that what we have been asked to do does not fit into our goals. At first this may seem like a selfish response. Yet if our priorities are straight (see PRIORITIES), then we will have already taken into account the needs and goals of others, at least those to which we are able to respond in a reasonably appropriate and effective manner. (see GOOD GOALS AND BAD GOALS)

Recently an executive of a large association called to invite me to be the featured speaker at their annual meeting. When I asked what was the purpose of the meeting his reply was, "It's our *annual* meeting." From this I think I was supposed to get the idea it was important and, therefore, I should be honored by the invitation.

"What is it that you want me to communicate? How can I help you?" I asked. "'Well, let us know what you think would be the most useful for us," he responded. The conversation ended by my asking him to go back to his committee to find out what was the purpose of my coming. If they had then come back and told me *why* they wanted me there, I would have been happy to accept or recommend someone whom I thought could do a better job if what they wanted did not lie in the area of my expertise. I didn't hear from them again!

Learning to say no also has a great deal to do with accepting your own capabilities. (see KNOW YOURSELF) A healthy self-estimate many times keeps us from accepting the task that someone else could do better, someone whose priorities and gifts are more relevant to the need at hand. (see GOD'S PURPOSE/MAN'S PLANS)

O

ORGANIZATIONS

Any time two people agree to work together on a common goal, you have an organization. People usually like to work together, but most of us don't like the idea of organization. There are a number of reasons for this:

— Organizations are bureaucratic.
— None of us likes to adhere to other people's agendas (see GOOD GOALS AND BAD GOALS)
— Organizations tend to generate rules and requirements, and most of us like to do our own thing.
— Organizations tend to stifle individual creativity.
— Organizations can quickly lose their original focus on needs — perpetuation tends to become purpose! Commitment to continuity dulls commitment to client.

But organizations are not only needful, they are useful. The trick is not to let them become self-serving institutions. By my definition an *organization* is a group of people who have come together to do a task outside of themselves.

Organizations can be terrible time wasters or wonderful time savers. The elements of an effective organization are:

Clear needs which cannot be met by individuals unorganized and alone.

Clear goals related to present needs which require regular reexamination and continual rebuilding of adaptive plans.

Motivated people who agree with the organization's goals, believe that they can make a contribution in meeting real needs of others and believe in the way organization is trying to get things done.

Adequate resources to do the job at hand.

Good communication within the organization so that each individual knows what he's supposed to do and has that information available to permit him to carry out his task.

An enabling climate. Only here is one able to effectively carry out plans.

In the above definition please notice: no mention is made of structure, style, or operations. These can all vary to suit the situation. If we understand this, we can get over the organization chart syndrome, bureaucratic pathology, and begin to see that there are many new creative ways of letting people work together for common goals.

To put it another way, the basic task of leadership of an organization is to create an environment within which expected things will happen. This is true of any organization, whether it be building automobiles, healing the sick, attempting to improve a neighborhood, or trying to cut down a next door neighbor's dead oak tree.

The local church is both an organization and a fellowship, and therefore there is a continual tension between enhancing people and getting the task of proclamation done. There is no easy way out of this dilemma, but it should be continually recognized and an attempt made

---

Task versus people is only one of the many creative tensions that are part of living. Virginia Mollenkott's *In Search of Balance* nicely spells out some of the tensions of accepting life as it is.

to strike a balance. As more and more organizations attempt to build enabling environments where individuals can fulfill their individual life goals as part of the organization's task, this same tension will grow. It's worth every bit of the anxiety it causes.

ORGANIZING IDEAS

One of the most effective time managing tools is getting ideas organized in useful patterns. When we talk about organizing we are really talking about *putting things in relationship* to each other. This might mean in terms of priorities, in terms of sequences of events, in terms of primary and supporting ideas, in terms of group relationships, in terms of familiar patterns, in terms of new and more useful patterns.

Part of creative thinking is to continually search for interrelationships between people, things, and events. The creative person believes that somewhere in the mess confronting him there is a unique system — a sequence or order.

To get ideas, things, or people organized, the first step is to describe and list all the possible elements one can think of as relevant. This is best done through the free association of ideas, either individually or with creativity groups, such as brainstorming or synectics sessions. The idea here is not to evaluate, but first to collect ideas. This can be done by either making handwritten or typed lists as fast as ideas come to you, by having a group sit around while one person writes down suggested ideas on an easel or a blackboard, or by just collecting other people's thoughts in a conference.

One very effective way is to have each member of the creativity or problem group write down his own idea on a 3 x 5 card as he makes the suggestion. (Slips of paper will work just as well, of course.) This speeds up the thought process and permits easy evaluation of the different ideas and arrangement of them whether on top of a table or a corkboard on the wall. (I call this "Spilling-your-brains-on-the-table".) Once a number of ideas have been produced, they can then be evaluated as to worth (see A, B, C's) or ranked according to time relationships by laying them face up on a table with "worth" ranked top to bottom and time from left to right.

There are many advantages to this technique over using a blackboard or easel:

— The process goes very rapidly because everyone is acting as "secretary."
— Everyone has a feeling of participation and is therefore more open to joint discussion and/or concensus.
— Ideas can be easily rearranged.
— Suggestions that don't fit because of magnitude, timing, or practicality are easily identified without offending the originator.

After ideas that have to do with the problem, the goal, or the situation facing you have been collected and related (together and to the goal situation), evaluate them by asking the following questions:

Is there any *relationship in time*? Which come first? Which come later?

Is there a *relationship of dependency*? Which of these things cannot happen unless the others happen?

Is there a *relationship of priority*? Which are the most important? Which are the most urgent?

Is there a *relationship of efficiency, effectiveness, efficaciousness*?

Are there *natural pairs or combinations*, things which just normally fit together? Is it "beautiful"?

Can the elements be *rearranged* in some new and more creative way to form a new unexpected solution or to uncover a previously undiscovered problem?

What gaps or missing elements are now evident? What new elements should be included as a result of trying to order these elements?

116

Results of such organization may be displayed in many ways. They can be arranged in check lists (see CHECK LISTS), displayed on organization charts, put down in logic diagrams (see DIAGRAMMING), described in "how-to-do-it" manuals or procedures, envisioned as future history, cast as scenarios of likely activities and events, or described as an accomplished fact at some future time, (e.g., the news, 20 years from now).

This is extremely effective as a way of group planning. (see PLANNING — HOW TO DO IT)

P

PEOPLE

What managing time is really all about is people — your fitting into their time needs and their fitting into yours. The whole reason for having clocks, schedules, calendars, plans and all the other tools we use for managing time is that there are a whole lot of people doing a whole lot of related things — all during the same time.

This basic idea of fitting people together like a big jig-saw puzzle can lead to an extremely mechanistic view of our people relationships. People can easily be viewed as parts of a vast machine which are either objects of our manipulation or against which we should be constantly on guard. There is much in our "rugged American individualism" and our frontier heritage which leads toward this view of people. It probably is possible to manage with such a view of people (or in spite of it!), but it is neither personally rewarding nor biblically honest.

In his description of the church the Apostle Paul described how we should relate to one another. He used the analogy of the human body . . . full of fingers and eyes and nose and toes and ears and legs and ankles. The body was incomplete without any one of them. The total body could not reject any one of its parts, nor could any one of its parts claim to *not* be part of the body. The whole body was truly sound only when all the parts were working together in harmony. (See Paul's first letter to the Church at Corinth — 12:12 ff.)

As we understand ourselves as part of a larger body, we are not only able to identify our gifts, but we also get our priorities straight (see PRIORITIES) and we begin to become most effective in our use of time.

It is impossible for me to disassociate myself and *my goals* from the selves and goals of other people. Only when I see myself as part of a larger whole, is there any meaning to life. (see PURPOSE)

St. Augustine is quoted as having said, "Love God and do as you please." What he was saying, of course, was that if I love God completely, *whatever* I please to do will please God. But how do I know if I love God? The Apostle John tells us that the way we know we love God is by the way we love our brothers. I check out my love relationship to God, the Father, by my love life with my brothers.

Friends, that's what it's all about! Any attempt to manage our time effectively, and therefore manage our lives, that misses this point, blows the whole ball game. (see KNOW YOURSELF and WHOLE MAN)

PERFECTIONISM

There are some people who never seem to be able to let go of a project. There is always one more chapter to "polish up," one "design improvement" to be made, one more set of figures to be checked. These are the perfectionists. They are found among engineers, artists, writers, housewives, junior executives (seldom middle managers and top managers), as well as a host of other people.

Perfectionism is a disease, because it goes beyond what is *needed*. (see CLOSURE) The world is an imperfect place. To obtain the first 90 percent toward perfection is usually easy. The last 5 percent is usually extremely costly.

Watch out for the perfectionists of this life, and watch out for yourself if you tend to be one.

Let me be quick to say that there are some things that need to be made as perfect as we can make them. (see EXCELLENCE) A good example is the extreme attention to detail, the constant check and doublecheck that goes into the space program. Here the risks are great. The payoff for success is large. The consequent drive for complete assurance is justified. And yet even here the requirements are the same. The basic criterion is to meet the understood *need* and no more.

The best way to control perfectionism is to use the clear, predefined goals (see GOALS) and a good follow-up or measurement plan. (see FOLLOW-UP) When the goal is reached (as noted by the measurement), move on to the next priority.

PHONE CALLS — INCOMING

Don't let incoming calls interrupt your involvement with other people. It is just as discourteous to let a telephone call interrupt as it would be to walk away from someone with whom you are talking.

If you have a secretary, and you are in a meeting or doing creative work, tell her to stop the calls (except from your boss!). Ask her to tell people why, and request that she tell them when you can be reached or when you will be back, and then keep your commitment. Most people will understand. (see PHONE CALLS — OUTGOING) Also ask her to find out what she can about what the person is seeking so you can be better prepared when you call back. She should also always get the best time and the proper number to call. It will save a great deal of look-up time and referrals.

Train your secretary, or whoever answers your phone, to have good telephone manners (make sure you have them yourself). Remember as far as the person calling is concerned he is calling *you*, and he will view you through whatever voice answers the telephone. The telephone company offers regular booklets and courses for secretaries, and other people who handle phones frequently. These stress courtesy and the handling of awkward situations. Every once in a while run a check on your own office by calling anonymously and asking for yourself just to see what happens. Train your callers by standardizing your scheduled time alloted to telephoning. (see STANDARD DAYS, WEEKS, MONTHS) People quickly learn when they can always get you!

If you are getting a number of calls at home during family or personal time, there are several things you might do:

— If it's personal time, have a member of the family screen the call before you take it.
— Install a mechanical answering device. They now cost less than $100.00.
— Use a telephone answering service.
— Have your calls automatically switched over to someone else in your organization.
— Unhook the phone.
— Don't answer! (The test of real self-discipline!)

Remember, the urgent is seldom important. (see URGENT OR IMPORTANT? and INDISPENSABLE — YOU ARE NOT) Don't get trapped by the tyranny of the telephone.

One exception. I never refuse a call from my wife or children. I let them know if I'm unable to talk, but first I find out their need. (see PRIORITIES)

P.S. If you haven't discovered the telephone reminder pad with the carbon copies in it, look for one. It automatically produces a record of all incoming calls, so that if you lose the slip of paper your secretary gives you, there is always a record in some other place. Your copy is also a handy place to note any agreements reached or commitments made in the course of the conversation.

PHONE CALLS — OUTGOING

The telephone is at once the greatest time saver and the greatest time waster many of us have. The trouble is it's so convenient, so at hand. How easy it is to say to yourself, "I wonder what Harry (or Mabel, or Bill, or Janet) thinks about that?" and grab the telephone. Or how often have you found yourself in the middle of a problem when a thought suddenly struck you and you reached for the telephone only to completely interrupt your own train of thought and never be able to recapture the creative moment you once had? (see INTERRUPTIONS)

Each person has to develop his own telephone style as a unique form of communication that takes skill and practice, but here are a few things you can do to save time.

Set a specific time during the day in which you are going to make phone calls. This can be useful both to you and to others. If you have a secretary, she knows when you will call people back, and she can assure callers that you will. If you are working at home or by yourself, you can be collecting ideas and noting things that will need to be talked about before you reach for the telephone in the midst of other things.

Make calls yourself. For most people it is more efficient to make the phone calls yourself rather than to have a secretary make them. This will depend upon your executive style, whether you are placing long distance or local calls, and whether you know the probability of the person's being there when you call. However, if you do ask a secretary to place your call, be available to take the call when she has made it.

Preorganize your thoughts. (see THREE BY FIVE CARD) Decide ahead of time what is the objective of the call, what data you're trying to get. Also, try to anticipate what the person you are going to call will want to know. Have this material available.

Use conference calls with a pre-agreed agenda. They're a lot less expensive than some trips, and they can be arranged very easily.

For long distance calls, *dial direct* rather than go through the operator. It will save time and money in the end. You can usually quickly discover when the person you want will be available or whether he is willing to call you back. If your call is going to take more than three minutes, you will make up the cost of the extra call because *two* direct dial calls cost less than one person-to-person call.

Make a record of agreements reached, and commitments made. Send the person called a copy, if it's important. Confirm commitments in a letter if it's vital to what you are doing together. Then you can be sure! (see COMMUNICATION)

PLANNING — DEFINED

Fail to plan, plan to fail.

If you've only got ten minutes to solve an urgent problem, take five minutes to plan how you're going to solve it.

124

There are a few people who over-plan, but they are mighty few.

Planning doesn't just have to do with big things. It has to do with little things, too. The good planning of little things eventually develops habits which become automatic plans in themselves. (see HABITS)

Planning is trying to discover how to accomplish goals *before* you commit yourself.

Planning is moving from the *now* to the *then,* from the "way things are" to the "way we want things to be."

Planning is trying to imagine the future as we would like it to be, and explaining how it could be.

For the Christian, planning is trying to understand God's will and respond to that understanding by our actions.

People have all kinds of misconceptions about planning. Planning is *not* deciding in advance every step we are going to take and then doggedly following those steps. Rather, planning is an arrow which points a direction of the future. You lay out the steps, take one step, and then replan. Planning thus becomes a road map toward the future. But unlike most road maps it's one which we can constantly improve as we move further and further toward that future.

Plan in advance how a job is done and it is already half-done.

PLANNING — HOW TO DO IT

Planning assumes a goal. Make sure your goal is measurable and accomplishable. (see GOALS)

State the goal. Picture the situation the way you want it to be. (see ORGANIZING IDEAS)

State the present situation. What are its characteristics? The present situation can be described both in terms of obstacles and opportunities for reaching the goal.

Now write down a number of things that might be useful steps toward the goal. (see ORGANIZING IDEAS) It is sometimes useful to ask the question: "what is the last thing that has to happen before the goal is accomplished?" Working backwards from the goal is a mind-clearing experience. If we try to work forward from our present situation, it's very easy to get bogged down by such statements as "we never did it that way before" or "we tried that, and it didn't work." Starting with a statement of where we want to be rather than where we are forces us from that.

After you have written down all the necessary steps, try to arrange them in order of sequence or priority. See where steps are missing. Allow for alternative approaches. Make sure you *have* a "Plan B." (see ALTERNATE PLANS)

Plans can be very elaborate, worked out in logic diagrams (see DIAGRAMMING), or they can just be check lists of things to do (see CHECK LISTS).

Make sure all the other people involved understand the plan and participate in it. Remember that by definition good plans like good goals are *your* plans while bad plans are *their* plans. (see GOOD GOALS AND BAD GOALS)

After you've laid out your plan, calculate the time, the money, and effort to do each step, and make sure you have the necessary resources. "For which of you, desiring to build a tower, does not first sit down and count the cost . . ." (Luke 14:28). If it won't work, replan.

And keep remembering you're in a *process*, a process of moving from where you are to where you want to be. Keep replanning! (see PLANNING — DEFINED)

Communicate your plans both to yourself and to others. Make them visible. Use charts, cards, calendars — any device to help you see your plans more completely and share them with others. (see DIAGRAMMING and FOLLOW-UP) And carefully define milestone and terminal events. (see CLOSURE)

P.S. Planning and problem-solving are closely related. For a more analytical approach, see PROBLEM-SOLVING.

PRAY YOUR PLANS

It is my firm conviction that one way to describe the purpose of every Christian is to "understand God's strategy and become a part of it." A major step toward such an understanding is certainly prayer.

I don't understand prayer. I don't understand how it works, but I'm convinced that it does. And in some way beyond my comprehension it is part of the total scheme of things, one of the laws of the universe. Different people have different ideas of when prayer takes place. To me the basic element is *consciously* calling ourselves into God's presence and addressing Him directly.

Planning requires the consideration of alternatives. Problem solving demands integration of experience and the present situation to find a way toward a solution. On the one hand, I believe that the quality of my everyday decisions is directly related to my relationship to my Christian brother. (see PEOPLE) On the other hand, I see myself under divine direction to ask for wisdom and guidance in all things.

This can work itself out in a number of ways:
— Praying over my things-to-do list each morning.
— Expecting that in times of prayer I will receive new ideas or recognize previously unnoticed problems.
— Periodically praying with family or associates about our (my) goals.

Each person can find his own style of seeking the guidance Christians are promised. The important thing is to *expect* that prayers and plans are part of a whole.

PRIORITIES

Basic to all time management is setting priorities. "First things first" is a slogan to which most of us give lip service. Setting priorities is, however, not always easy. Good priorities demand first that we have *clear goals* and that we have "prioritized" these. (see GOALS)

Priorities basically have to do with the *when* of our lives.

There are lifetime priorities, generation priorities, yearly priorities, monthly priorities, weekly priorities, and daily priorities.

Investing your time is investing your life. For the Christian that time investment must be based on some biblical priorities. The order of those biblical priorities is:

1) Commitment to Christ.
2) Commitment to the Body of Christ, His Church, and the people who make it up.
3) Commitment to the work of Christ.

Many Christians have the order mixed up. They forget that Christianity is basically a *relationship*. God is much more interested in what we are than what we accomplish, and what we *are* is measured by our relationships — kindness, righteousness, lovingness, goodness, are all attributes we have in a relationship to other persons. (see ASSUMPTIONS)

At first this will seem a strange way to set up our lifetime priorities. Most of us think of our *work,* our *profession,* or our *life calling* as that which is the most important part of our lives. But that drive toward professional accomplishment can destroy our relationships with others and thus destroy our very being.

The concept of giving higher priority to the Body of Christ than to the work we are doing certainly gives a high priority to our family. Take a look at your calendar. If there are no dates with your children, your wife, or your total family, you've missed one of the major priorities. (see FILL UP YOUR CALENDAR)

But assuming we have a set of Christian priorities, how do we sort out the various goals and things we have to do? The first step is to list all we want to accomplish in a lifetime, or in a year, or in a month, or in a week, or in a day. Begin to rank them. (see MANAGING YOUR TIME)

One easy way of doing this is to not attempt to put them all in one, two, three order but rather to classify them as A, B, or C. (see A, B, C's)

Concentrate on the A's and do those first. If two projects seem about equal, it may not make any difference which one you do first, but *do* one of them. Begin now! (see CLOSE DECISIONS) The B's and C's may have to wait indefinitely. Remember, however, that setting priorities is part of the goal-setting and planning *process*. A review of priorities next week may uncover a new set. (see LITTLE THINGS — THAT BECOME BIG ONES)

PROBLEM SOLVING

There is a close relationship between planning and problem-solving. In each case there is a recognition that an *action is required;* there are a *variety of approaches* from which we might select to carry out the action; there is an *element of doubt* about the outcome; there is the *element of time* to carry out the actions; and there is a need to recognize that there are *steps required* for successful action.

I once made the statement to some good friends that the systems engineer could handle any problem. It took me awhile to point out to my incredulous friends that I didn't say *solve* any problem, but only that it could be handled. There is a big difference.

There is a standard approach to any problem which may not solve the problem, but which will at least help us get a handle on it.

1. *Understand what needs to be done:*
   — State the problem or the goal as you understand it. Write down all your *assumptions* about the situation or the goal.
   — Break it down into logical elements. These might be different areas to be covered, products to be sold,

amounts to be achieved, kinds of people to be reached. (see DIVIDE AND CONQUER)
  — Analyze each part and describe it.
  — Set an *accomplishable* and *measurable* goal for each part. (see GOALS)
2. *Devise an overall strategy or approach.*
  — What is the situation in which the problem exists? What is the "climate" for solution?
  — Who else will have to be involved?
  — To what larger problem does this problem relate?
  — How much time do we have to solve the problem?
  — On the basis of the answers to the above questions, what is the best place to begin?
3. *Compare the task with known experience.*
  — Do we know of another approach or solution that has worked in a similar situation? Consider it.
  — What methods, approaches, or solutions have been tried but found harmful? Reject these.
  — Do we know of an approach or solution which has been tried and found useless and thus should be avoided? Avoid this.
  — If we know of no approach toward solution, what research or analysis should be carried out to find an approach? Research is the supplying of missing experience. (see RESEARCH)
4. *Make a plan to do the task.* (see PLANNING — HOW TO DO IT and ORGANIZING IDEAS)
  — Select from previous experience or methods the approaches and solutions to be taken. Develop a rich set of alternatives. Make a decision among them.
  — Identify steps toward reaching the goal for each part for which you have set a goal.
  — Decide on ways for measuring progress for each step. (see FOLLOW-UP)
  — Estimate the time needed for each step. Consider the need for the worst case (everything goes wrong!), the best case, and decide which is the most likely amount of time needed.

- Estimate the finances needed for each step. (Use best and worst case here, too!)
- Estimate the facilities needed for each step. What are you going to need besides money and people?
- Estimate the people needed for each step. Who else are you going to need to help you in this task? What kind of people are they? What are their goals? Will they "buy in" on yours? Are they committed to the task? How should they be organized?
- Play the DEADLY ENEMY game. What are all the things wrong with this plan that will cause it not to work?
- If one or more of these estimates indicates the plan won't work, replan or seek another solution (which may eventually mean modifying the goal).

5. *Gather resources to carry out the plan.*
- Get the money together.
- Mobilize the people, which includes staffing and organizing and any necessary training. (see GOOD GOALS AND BAD GOALS)
- Bring your facilities together.

6. *Carry out the plan.*
- Start working your plan.
- Measure results as you go along. (see FOLLOW-UP)
- Correct deviations from plan or modify the plan. Work your plan. Don't let your plan work you! So often we find people have agreed on follow-up systems and then fail to use them. You're bound to meet the unexpected. Try to take advantage of it. (see MISTAKES)
- Keep measuring results.
- Consolidate gains. Make sure you plan for success and count on using your success to build for the future. Don't be like the people who came together after a year's drought in Kansas to pray for rain and discovered that only one small girl had brought an umbrella.

131

— When results measured match the goal definition, the goal has been achieved. (see CLOSURE)
7. *Use the results.*
   — The goal should be seen as part of a larger task.
   — The results should be used (feedback) for another task. Share what you have learned with others. (And don't leave out the things that went wrong!)

PROCRASTINATION

Why do we procrastinate? Why do we fail to act? Most of the time it is basically fear.
   — We are afraid of evaluation, afraid we'll make a mistake, and be criticized by others, afraid the result is not perfect (see PERFECTIONISM) and we'll criticize ourselves!
   — We are afraid we are not the ones to make the decision.
   — Sometimes we're afraid of completing the job. We wonder what we'll do next!
   — Other times the alternatives appear to be equal, and we vascillate between them. (see CLOSE DECISION)
When faced with procrastination make a list of the alternatives (including taking no action). List the pluses and minuses for each. Then make a decision, and forget it. Even if your decision is to do nothing, by assuring yourself you have weighed the options, you have faced your fears and moved ahead.

PROPHETS IN THEIR OWN COUNTRY

Have you ever noticed how we continually tend to picture people as they were when we first knew them?

I've attemped to diagram some of these steps in an earlier workbook entitled, *God's Purpose/Man's Plans* (MARC, Monrovia, California, 1971).

This is particularly true of individuals as they join organizations. A young man may enter a company, and the impression he makes during the first year will last with his associates for the rest of his time there. Sometimes the only way he can break out of the mold which they have constructed for him is to leave.

The same thing can happen to the individual in his perception of himself. I remember one time after I had worked in the area of aircraft instrumentation for a number of years, an ad hoc group of engineering section heads had been assembled to write a large high-priority proposal. My part of the task was the instrumentation. Late one evening I asked the group how the information might best be displayed to the crew of the aircraft. "Ed, *you're* the display expert. You decide!" was the reply. I suddenly realized this was the first time I had ever seen myself as an *expert*. At home they knew me too well!

In his own perception, and many times in the perception of others, the prophet has no honor in his own country. We just don't imagine the boy next door could really be anything else. (Behind every successful man there stands an amazed mother-in-law.)

Recognizing the "no honor in your own country" syndrome can get us past all kinds of communicating frustrations. When you are in your own familiar territory, maybe the technique one of my friends advocates will work: "The way to sell your idea is to plant it in someone else's head. When he proposes it, you oppose it, and then it will get passed."

People are people after all, aren't they?

PROVERBS

"A stitch in time saves nine."
"Haste makes waste."
Both proverbs. Both true. Both contradictory. Proverbs

are true most of the time. They are the result of the combined experience of many men through the years. They need to be put in their proper perspective and used at the proper time. Much of the advice given in this book about time management is like these proverbs. It needs to be appropriately applied. Any ideas for an "appropriateness rule" or concept? (see PROBLEM SOLVING)

"A man's mind plans his way but the Lord directs his steps" (Prov. 16:9).

PURPOSE

If you don't care where you're going, any road will get you there, and it really doesn't make any difference how much time you take.

Purpose — the why of what we are doing — is not necessarily measurable in itself, but it sets a clear direction.

What a sad thing it is to reach that point when most of life lies behind us and to discover we really don't know the *why* of what has gone before.

Our purpose in living is the stuff on which our goals are built, and without goals in life we can never effectively manage our time. (see GOALS)

"Live life, then, with a due sense of responsibility, not as men (and women) who do not know the meaning and purpose of life but as *those who do.* Make the best use of your time, despite all the difficulties of these days."
— Ephesians 5:15, 16 (Phillips)

Q

QUALITY TIME

I have a good friend who is also a very prominent person. He travels and speaks all over the world, and meets hundreds of new people each week. But he has that charmingly wonderful ability to see you again in a crowd of people, take your hand, and for the few brief minutes he is with you to give you his complete, undivided attention.

It isn't *how much* time you have to give, but the *quality* of the time you give that really makes you an effective person, both for yourself and for others. Being in the presence of others doesn't mean you're really *with* them. You may spend one hour with your six-year-old while he is playing in the back yard and not build as much into his life as if you had spent fifteen minutes of really concentrating on him, understanding and relating to him.

Giving quality time takes concentration and practice. (see HABITS) Concentration can be sharpened by a strong belief that what we are doing meets our goals for ourselves and others. (see LISTENING)

To get quality time for yourself be certain there is adequate time to do what has to be done. Interruptions or the foreshortening of a needed block of time can really ruin what you have done up to that time. (see INTERRUPTIONS) Make sure you're working in the right environment. (see ENVIRONMENT) If the environment you're in is not conducive to quality time, change the environment.

Look ahead to times when you are going to need blocks of time for creative work, and put those on the calendar.

QUESTIONS

I once worked for a man whose entire management technique seemed to be centered around one question — "Why?" If you made a proposal to him, his first question was "Why?" When you answered that, his next question was "Why?" And so it went. It didn't make any difference how well acquainted he was with the problem or how expert he was in the area, that simple quote "why?" drove you to the wall.

I don't recommend this as a standard operating procedure for dealing with other people, but it points up the value of asking questions. (see ASK)

Too often we have right answers to the wrong questions. The right question can be more important than the right answer.

Questions should come at the beginning of the time-saving process when we are trying to define what it is we want to do, when we are collecting information, and when we are trying to evaluate which way to go. Questions carefully written for a broader distribution can help everyone get started. The standard news reporter's stand-bys, "Who, what, why, when, where, how?" are all applicable:

— Ask *why* and you may eliminate it.

— Ask *where* and you may find a better place to do it.

— Ask *when* and you may find a better schedule.

— Ask *who* and you are likely to find the most appropriate person to do it.

— Ask *what* and you may find you are working on the wrong problem.

— Ask *how* and you may find a better solution.

It is helpful to develop a check list of standard questions (see CHECK LISTS) about your operations.

It is also important to know when to *stop* asking questions. If no new information is coming back or if there is a tendency to repeat the same answer in a different form, that is a good time to stop. Also watch out for the impact your questions are having on the individual or individuals being questioned. Make sure they are perceived at the correct level. Too often a technical question is perceived on a personal level, and the individual is threatened by it rather than encouraged. (see COMMUNICATION)

People who ask a lot of questions are not always popular, but it is an effective way to learn. (see ASK)

RELIEF VALVES

We all need relief valves. They can save a lot of time that we would normally take cleaning up the mess caused by personal explosions.

When we installed a new hot water heater recently I discovered a local ordinance which says that there has to be a relief valve hooked up somewhere in the water system. If for some reason the thermostat doesn't turn off the gas under the boiler, and the boiler is so hot it is ready to explode, the valve will pop off, and pressure will be relieved. Things may stay just as hot under the boiler, but at least it won't blow up all over the house.

One of the most effective, long-range relief valves is to recognize what causes the build up of pressure. If you see, by your calendar, that you are in for a few heavy weeks or too many late nights, block some relief valve time into your calendar. This might be a half day, whole day, or extended week-end. Take yourself ˙out of your normal situation. Place yourself in a situation in which past experience has shown you can forget what is going on. (see KNOW YOURSELF) This may mean a day alone at the beach, or the mountains, a day with your family, or something like a week-end away with your husband or wife. It's a big help if couples will discuss their future schedules together to identify where the overload problems are and schedule in breaks in the routine.

In addition to the count-to-ten pressure reliever with which most of us are familiar, there are some others:

— Staying *ahead* of your work is a good way to relieve the pressure of schedules. By scheduling a completion time 10-20 percent ahead, you have the peace of knowing there's time to recover if things go wrong.
— Doing the hard things first, particularly if they have a great deal of emotional content, will relieve the subterranean emotions which tend to plague us in difficult situations.
— Getting enough sleep is a must. Know how long you can get along with a reduced amount.
— Do the difficult tasks in phases. Often a "first draft" will get you 80 percent of the way along. Time for "topping off" the finished product can be better foreseen, and meeting the deadline seems less of a task. (see STAY AHEAD)

Admitting and verbalizing the causes for your own irritations, be they lack of sleep, over-work, over-stress, or what have you, helps others from getting emotional with you and triggering unexpected explosions.

Facing up to the fact you really *can't* do all the things you scheduled and that some of them need to be postponed is probably the best relief valve of all. This can be a humbling experience but the rewards in personal well-being are great. (see RESCHEDULE)

RESCHEDULE

Your schedule and your life will be continually interrupted! Work out ways to reschedule those things which

140

you've been forced to postpone. This would include not only tasks, but time with others and time with God. It's surprising how accountable we will be to something like Rotary, where if we miss four meetings we're out; we have to keep making them up. And yet at the same time we often don't transfer this concept to making up missed time with others or with the Lord.

Don't feel guilty about it. Reschedule it!

RESEARCH

In spite of all the other fancy definitions you'll find for it, research is basically the attempt to supply missing experience. We have a problem facing us, a goal to reach, a decision to make. Since we all make such analysis on the basis of past experience (ours and others) as long as we feel we have adequate experience, we are ready to move ahead. If we don't feel we have enough experience, we make guesses or go by hunch (a fast way to obtain experience!), or if we have the time (and the common sense) we do some research. This "research" may be just to make inquiries, or it may be much more formal. In any event, what we need are "facts" we can believe in.

It is true that some people embark on research for research's sake or because of an academic interest, but most of the research done is started because we don't know how to reach a goal we want to obtain, or we're trying to find a better way of reaching that same goal.

Asking questions is research. (see ASK) Going through problem-solving techniques uncovers the need for research. (see PROBLEM SOLVING)

Research is important. Don't neglect it. Put aside time to do it, but remember, the question is not, "How well you know something?" but rather, "What difference does it make?"

RESOURCES

The mature Christian has come to realize that the walk of faith assumes the acceptance of many paradoxes. God is sovereign, yet men have freedom. God is at work in the world, yet He intends men to be responsible. Capabilities and talents are gifts from God, yet we are called upon to develop them. Perhaps it is best summed up in the mystery of prayer. God knows all that is happening and will happen, yet He commands that we should pray and gives us positive assurance that our praying makes a difference.

Christian maturity also sees the world as a whole. There are no sinful things, only sinful people. What secular men have learned about how the world "works" and how humans behave is also God's gift to His Church. One of those gifts is a growing understanding of how leadership can function more effectively in a world of increasingly complex organizations.

But the mystery remains. No amount of management know-how, no reading of books or attendance at seminars will guarantee "results." God does His work *His* way. He expects us to find our ultimate dependency in Him.

There is a growing realization that "management" has a valid and essential role in the operation of Christian organizations. However, not a great deal has been written specifically for the Christian organization and the Christian leader.

This list of "resources" has been prepared for Christian leaders, men whom God has placed in the role of manager. Leadership usually assumes an organization of some kind, so leadership has to do with the management of organizations and Christian leadership with Christian organizations.

Books

There is a wide variety of books available on leadership management and management skills. It is a good idea to build up a small library of four or five that will meet your present need and be a good reference to you. (It's also very helpful to have a book you can loan to someone whom you want to encourage toward better management performance.)

Personal Management

The Effective Executive by Peter Drucker (Harper & Row, New York, 1967) is one of the best. Drucker is the recognized dean of management trainers. This book is designed to help the individual improve his insights into people and helping others achieve their goals while achieving his own.

The Time Trap — Managing Your Way Out by Alec Mackenzie (Amacom, New York, 1972) begins with the problem of managing yourself as a key to managing your time.

How To Get More Done in Less Time by Joseph D. Cooper (Doubleday & Company, Garden City, revised 1971) is almost 500 pages of ideas on how to be more personally effective in your work.

Management Styles in Transition by Glenn A. Bassett (American Management Association, New York, 1966) discusses how social changes, advanced technology, restricted action, and pressure affect the manager's job and what he must do to develop new and sophisticated skills to meet the demands of organizational dynamics.

The Uncommon Man: The Individual in the Organization by Crawford H. Greenewalt (McGraw-Hill Book Company, Inc., New York, 1959). The author points out the relative scarcity of truly outstanding leaders — and stresses the need for providing proper incentives to draw them into positions of heavy responsibility.

Organizational Management

The Management Profession by Louis A. Allen (McGraw-Hill Book Company, Inc., New York, 1964) is devoted to the elements of management as a profession. Divides management into four functions and establishes nineteen

143

areas of management activity. Also provides applicable principles of management under related activities.

Tough-Minded Management by J. D. Batten (American Management Association, New York, 1963) is a practical and personal approach to management's growing need for tough-minded executives who have the vitality to make things happen — and at the same time demand facts, blueprints for action and realistic controls.

The Priest As Manager by James Deegan, Jr., (Bruce Publishing Company, St. Paul, Minn., 1969) is excellent. (Good stuff for Protestants too!)

Building a Dynamic Corporation Through Good Organizational Development by Robert Blake and Jane Mouton (Addison Wesleyen, 1969). It deals with the tension of the task versus personal orientation in organizations.

Organization Development, Its Nature, Origin, and Prospects by Warren Bennis (Addison Wesleyen) is a good introduction to emerging theories of organizational development.

Management by Exception by Lester R. Bittel (McGraw-Hill Book Company, Inc., New York, 1964) is useful for its "laundry list" of management functions and subfunctions that lend themselves to monitoring and measurement.

The Practice of Management by Peter F. Drucker (Harper & Row, New York, 1954) is accepted by many as a landmark text in management. It synthesizes basic concepts developed earlier and sets forth practical information on major industrial firms.

Managing Your Time by Ted W. Engstrom and Alec Mackenzie (Zondervan, Grand Rapids, 1967) is written from a Christian world view. It is a general introduction to management theory with emphasis on time management. Available in paperback.

Management by Motivation by Saul W. Gellerman (American Management Association, New York, 1968) is in essence a book of management development aimed at the staffman middle manager or top manager to help him improve his skills in this process. Translates some of the

144

psychologist's tools into practical language for the lay manager — for example, his risk-competence diagram for use in selection of personnel.

Principles of Management by Harold Koontz and Cyril O'Donnell (Fourth edition, McGraw-Hill Book Company, New York, 1968) is an orderly presentation summarizing the thinking of many leaders in the development of management as an organized body of knowledge. Includes several useful definitions of often-used management terms. Frequently used as a university text but useful to the businessman.

The Human Side of Enterprise by Douglas McGregor (McGraw-Hill Book Company, Inc., New York, 1960) compares two theories of human behavior. Theory X assumes the average worker doesn't like to work and does so under threat of punishment. Theory Y assumes that work is natural to man and motivation is dependent on how well the human needs — physiological, social, egotistic — can be satisfied.

An important section of the book is devoted to an analysis of leadership involving: (1) the characteristics of the leader; (2) the needs and other personal characteristics of the followers; (3) the characteristics of the organization; and (4) the social, political, and economic environment.

Management by Objectives by George S. Odiorne (Pitman, New York, 1965). There are a number of basic theories of management. The theory of "management by objective" holds forth the concept that if we organize all of our analyses of our progress against the goals and objectives which we have set both as an organization and for individuals that the rest of the management functions will find their proper place. This book is particularly useful for Christian and other nonprofit organizations.

Managing Our Work by John W. Alexander (Inter-Varsity Press, Downers Grove, Illinois, 1972) is written by the President of Inter-Varsity Christian Fellowship. Applies clearly articulated Biblical principles to management, particularly planning, execution and review. Gives specific helps on how-to-do-it.

Setting Goals

Goal Setting: Key to Organizational Effectiveness by Charles L. Hughes (American Management Association, New York 1965). This McKinsey award-winning book describes how overall objectives can be broken down into subgoals for managers and employees at all levels.

God's Purpose/Man's Plans by Edward R. Dayton (MARC, Monrovia, California, 1971) is a workbook particularly aimed at the manager involved in Christian organizations. It gives program instruction on motivating people toward goal setting and then has two sections, one on planning and one on problem solving.

Goals Analysis by Robert F. Mager (Fearon, Belmont, California) is a stimulating discussion on the problems of "Fuzzies" (fuzzy goals) and how to form them up. Very good self-instruction book.

Integrating the Individual and the Organization by Chris Argyris (John Wiley and Sons, New York, 1964) discusses at length the continuing management problem of resolving individual goals with the requirements of corporate objectives.

Organizing

Organization by Ernest Dale (American Management Association, New York, 1967) covers all aspects of organization: line and staff, general staff, the chief executive and his staff, reorganizatiton, international operations and the impact of computers on organization. Many organization charts are included.

Planning

Parish Planning by Lyle E. Schaller (Abingdon, 1971) is subtitled "How to Get Things Done in Your Church"

146

and not only contains its own good bibliography, but is an excellent basic source book.

Problem Solving

The Rational Manager by Charles H. Kepner and Benjamin B. Tregoe (McGraw-Hill Book Company, New York, 1965) sets forth a systematic approach to problem solving and decision making. Describes procedures for analyzing problems, making decisions and for preventing potential problems.

Church Fights: Managing Conflict in the Local Church by Speed Leas and Paul Kittlaus includes a very adequate discussion on procedures pastors may follow on solving problems (Westminster Press, 1973).

Introducing Change

The Human Side of Planning by David W. Ewing (Macmillan, New York, 1969). This is one of the few books on planning that deals with all the obstacles to making good planning work for you. It lays out in honest detail the type of human interaction that is needed in order to implement any plan.

The Change Agent by Lyle E. Schaller (Abingdon, 1972) talks about the human side of planning from the Christian organizational viewpoint, and particularly the Church. Highly recommended for any pastor or Christian leader who wants to be an agent of change in his church.

Concepts

Human Behavior in Organizations by Leonard R. Sayles and George Strauss (Prentice Hall, Inc., Englewood Cliffs, New Jersey, 1966) integrates the relevant organizational behavior research with a thorough knowledge of the realities of organizational operating problems. Assists in obtaining a genuine understanding of what it is like to work, to manage, and to resolve conflicting pressures inside an organizational structure.

The Systems Approach by C. West Churchman (Delta

Publishing Company, New York, 1968) is an extremely useful introduction to the entire idea of systems and how they affect organizational thought. Although not written from a Christian viewpoint, it recognizes the fact that all systems thinking must eventually end up with the consideration of *value*.

Rapid Reading/Comprehension Building

The Now Student by Edward Spargo (Jamestown Publishers, Providence, 1971) is probably the best complete reading and learning skills book available.
Rapid Reading With a Purpose by Ben E. Johnson (Regal Press) provides assistance to greater efficiency in reading habits.

Secretaries

Your secretary may need some help too. The following is a list of secretarial handbooks that might be useful:
Complete Secretary's Handbook by Lillian Doris and Besse May Miller (Prentice-Hall, 1970).
Secretarial Study Guide published by NSA (National Secretaries Association), Kansas City.
Executive Secretary's Handbook by Pauline Engel (Prentice-Hall, 1965).
The last chapter of Mackenzie's *The Time Trap* also has some excellent material on working with secretaries.

Games

Gaming by Dennis Benson (Abingdon, 1971). A book with two records included on the "fine art of creating simulation/learning games for religious education."

Magazines

Business Week (Published by McGraw-Hill, Inc., 1221 Avenue of the Americas, New York 10020) is a good magazine to keep abreast of what others are doing in the world of "getting things done." It is probably most useful for those managers who are involved in organizations which have quite a bit of intercourse with secular organizations.

Church Management: The Clergy Journal (115 N. Main Street, Mount Holly, North Carolina 28120) covers a wide range of topics, mostly of interest to church business administrators.

Harvard Business Review (Soldiers Field, Boston, Massachusetts 02163) is expensive, but well worth it for managers of large organizations who may want to keep abreast of advanced thinking in management in Western societies.

Your Church (Its Planning, Building, Equipment, and Administration) is available from The Religious Publishing House (122 Old York Road, Jenkintown, Pennsylvania 19406).

Workbooks

Your denomination or organization may have some workbooks that will be useful to you and also useful if you want to do some training. Outside the regular organization, these workbooks may be useful:

God's Purpose/Man's Plans by Ed Dayton is a four part workbook and text on relating goals and planning and problem solving to God's purposes for man. It begins with two programmed instructions. (MARC, 919 West Huntington Drive, Monrovia, California 91016, 1971, 58 pages, $2.00 single copy.)

Christian Leadership Development is a series of thirty-six course outlines developed by Peter Wiwcharuck. Although intended as outlines, there is a great deal of meat in the material and many biblical illustrations you can use. Write Mr. Peter Wiwcharuck, 6110 48A Avenue, Ladner (Delta), British Columbia, Canada. This 309 page book is well worth the $5.00 cost.

Management Training Manual is a self-study workbook written under the classical management training headings, with emphasis on "how-to" techniques. Includes four cassette tapes on leadership by Howard Hendricks

($35.00, Campus Crusade for Christ, c/o Mr. Steve Douglass, Arrowhead Springs, San Bernardino, California 92414.)

Cassettes

Even if you don't like to sit and listen to other people talk, portable cassette recorders make it possible for you to do two things at once. They are particularly useful while you are driving your car, waiting for others, or doing some manual work which doesn't require you to to talk to anyone. There are a number of cassette series available:

Campus Crusade for Christ has a series of varying quality. Write to them for their catalog. The ones by Howard Hendricks are particularly good. You might also be interested in the ones on management by Steve Douglass.

The Nation's Business offers a series called "Executive Seminars in Sound." Write to Nation's Business, 1615 H Street, Northwest, Washinton D. C. 20006. The cost is $7.50 a piece.

Word Publishers, Waco, Texas, has a number of cassettes on management and leadership. Write for their catalog.

Managing Time by R. Alec Mackenzie is available from the Institute for Leadership, 10 Kipp Street, Chappaqua, New York 10514. Nine cassettes and workbook published by Advanced Management Research, $295.

American Bible Society has the Bible recorded on tapes. Write to American Bible Society, 1865 Broadway, New York, New York 10023.

You will also notice that there are many advertisements for management training tapes in both Christian and secular magazines. Be selective here. Choose the ones that seem to meet your needs.

Newsletters

The advantage of a monthly newsletter is that you usually get four to eight pages of material conveniently digested for you which you can then absorb at your own pace. Some newsletters are free; others cost a nominal amount.

The Christian Leadership Letter is a four to six-page monthly letter made available free of charge by World Vision International. It combines philosophical discussion on basic principles of management and leadership along with practical "how-to" ideas including various reproducible charts and check lists that you can use. The letter is edited by Ted Engstrom and Ed Dayton. Write *Christian Leadership Letter*, 919 West Huntington Drive, Monrovia, California 91016.

Notes and Quotes is a four-page newsletter of comment on management and employee relations and is published by the Connecticut General Life Insurance Company, Hartford, Connecticut 06115. It is available to you free of charge. One of the nice advantages of this newsletter is that it has condensations of reprints and company booklets which you can then order free of charge if you would like to have them.

The Parish Paper is produced by Lyle E. Schaller, Author of *Parish Planning* and *The Change Agent*. The primary criterion for subject matter "Would the governing board or program committee of the local church be interested in discussing this at their meeting next month?" It comes out monthly and is available for $5.00 per year for five copies. Write Yokefellow Institute, 530 N. Brainard Street, Naperville, Illinois 60540.

The Royal Bank of Canada Monthly Letter. Post Office Box 6001, Montreal, Quebec, Canada. Covers a wide range of management topics. Free on request.

Probe — a potpourri containing frequent references to games and simulations available for use with names and addresses. (Department of Communication, Christian Associates of Southwest Pennsylvania, 220 Grant Street, Pittsburgh, Pennsylvania 15241. $5.00 per year.)

Recycle — a potpourri of imaginative ideas on reusing almost anything for Christian education and communication purposes, with frequent references to games and simulations available, with names and addresses. (*Recycle*, Box 12811, Pittsburgh, Pennsylvania 15241. Published ten times yearly. $5.00 per year.

Films

Enquire at your university, large public library and management associations for training films. Write to *Modern Talking Picture Service, Inc.* (2323 New Hyde Park Road, New Hyde Park, New York, 11040) for a catalog of *free-loan* training films.

Management Associations

The most well known management association, of course, is the *American Management Association* with headquarters in New York. Individual membership costs $75 per year, organizational membership is $150. For this, you get a wide variety of publications which may or may not suit your needs. Write the American Management Association, 135 West 50th Street, New York, New York 10020, for further information.

The *American Institute of Management* may be of interest to some. Write to 125 W. 38th Street, New York, New York 10016, for more information.

Be on the lookout for local management or leadership associations of which you might want to become a part (or start your own!)

Training Seminars

There are a wide variety of training seminars available, most of which are put on through the resources of your local university. The easiest way to find these out is to place a telephone call to the nearest large university and ask for their industrial relations or management training center, and make inquiry as to how you can learn more. They vary in cost and value, and it is usually a good idea to try to find someone who has been to one before. *Yokefellow Institute*, 920 Earlham Drive, Richmond, Indiana 47374, sponsors a number of workshops for pastors in a wide variety of subjects. Ask to be put on their mailing list.

The Church Consultation Service, 177 North Madison Avenue, Pasadena, California 91101, offers both regular and special training seminars.

World Vision International, 919 West Huntington Drive, Monrovia, California 91016, sponsors two-day Managing Your Time seminars aimed primarily at Christian leaders. The first day deals with how to go about gaining mastery of your own personal time management. The second day of the two-day seminar tries to apply these personal concepts to the management of the Christian organization.

Campus Crusade for Christ has week-long management seminars for pastors. Write to Mr. Steve Douglass, Arrowhead Springs, San Bernardino, California 92404, for information about whether they might be having a seminar in your area.

Olan Hendric's Management Skills Seminars, Box 368, 672 Conestoga Road, Villanova, Pennsylvania 19085, are three-day seminars which introduce the Christian Executive to management concepts and also include a speed reading course.

Resource Centers and Enablers

Enquire at your nearest university and seminary for resource people. Don't overlook denominational resources. Those published by the major denominations have a wide variety of materials and individuals available. It is usually worth a phone call to denominational headquarters to locate the right person.

The Yearbook of American Churches (Abingdon Press, C. H. Jacquet, Jr., Editor) will give addresses. You will have to ask information for phone numbers.

The Association for Creative Charge in Religious Organizations, 521 N. 20th Street, Birmingham, Alabama 35203, is a national group of trainers and persons interested in church development. It includes many highly trained and certified management trainers.

The Church Consultation Service mentioned above can also be helpful and make recommendations.

S

SACRED OR SECULAR

There is no such thing. It's a dichotomy built into our Christian thinking that ought to undergo radical surgery wherever it is found.

All of life is sacred. All men are sacred in God's sight. There are no sinful things, only sinful persons.

"And *whatever* you do, in word or deed, do everything in the name of the Lord Jesus, giving thanks to God the Father through Him" (Col. 3:17).

And this applies to our time. It is all sacred. God is just as pleased when I am giving high quality time to my son as He is when I am in church singing in the choir.

What a relief!

SCHEDULING

Scheduling is the time sequencing of our plans.

Scheduling is taking into account the plans and goals of others and fitting our schedule into theirs.

Scheduling needs to be done, not only with the calendar, but by placing tasks and events in relationship to one another so we can understand dependencies.

Investigate the various scheduling tools available for personal time scheduling and program time scheduling. There is good pay-off in finding systems that will display the schedule, uncover problems, and permit you to reschedule when problems arise. (see ORGANIZING IDEAS and CALENDARS)

Make sure that whatever system you use is not too elaborate, but make sure you have something.

Scheduling systems include pocket appointment calendars, desk calendars, and wall calendars, program charts (PERT, etc.) check lists, things-to-do list. Look for systems which will integrate all of the things you are doing in your total life. (see WHOLE MAN) You will be continually tempted to violate your own priorities. Keep control of violations by re-examining those priorities as well as your goals continually. Schedules should always be carefully labeled, "subject to change!"

SLEEP

I never cease to be amazed at the wonder of sleep nor to agonize over the lack of it. I am one of those people who needs seven and a half hours every day to work at an optimum effectiveness. I wish I could get along on five or even six hours a day, but I can't. The moment I forget that, I am in trouble.

There are evidently all different qualities of sleep (have you ever heard yourself say, "I *really* had a good sleep last night"?) Learn what contributes to your getting a good night's sleep. (see KNOW YOURSELF) Keep such contributions to your well-being planted into your schedule. When you see that you are falling behind, figure out what you need to do to catch up, and put that on the schedule too. Or reschedule.

156

SOLUTIONS LOOKING FOR PROBLEMS

The world is full of pat solutions. Too often, I am afraid, I start giving someone a solution to his problem before he has completely explained what his problem is. People tend to organize around solutions rather than around problems. This is quite natural since most solutions tend to be products, services, or ways of doing things. Many consulting firms fall in this category. They have standard ways of solving your problem, regardless of whether or not they completely understand the problem you're facing.

There are some real dangers in this approach of applying solutions to problems. The first is that too often we throw the baby out with the bath water. The solution not only kills the bad things we are doing, it kills the good things too. The second danger is that the solution will cover only part of the problem.

A much better way is to examine the problem from the inside and work our way out. (see PROBLEM-SOLVING) Usually an existing solution needs to be modified for our particular problem or goal.

The next time you are offered a solution to a problem, start with two assumptions: First, assume that it may be part of the answer. Next, *see what has to be* modified to adapt it to your situation. (see CREATIVE TIME)

And don't forget the DEADLY ENEMY game. . . .

STANDARD DAYS, WEEKS AND MONTHS

One of the best ways to make effective use of our time and the time of others is to have regularly scheduled times for doing different things. By arranging these recurring times into standard days, standard weeks, standard months, or all three we help to get ourselves into good work habits and to have places into which to put certain things automatically.

A standard day for an executive might include:

8:00 – 8:30	Discuss day with secretary, replan day.
8:30 – 10:00	Correspondence.
10:00 – 10:30	Return & make telephone calls.
10:30 – 12:00	Scheduled meetings.
12:00 – 1:30	Lunch
1:30 – 4:30	Open for others or special tasks.
4:30 – 5:00	Plan next day.

A standard day for a housewife (with kids in school) might look something like this:

7:00 – 8:00	Get breakfast and children and husband off to school and work.
8:00 – 8:30	Devotional and planning time for the day.
8:30 – 9:30	Clean up.
9:30 – 11:00	Daily project (such as laundry, shopping, painting, sewing, etc.).
11:00 – 12:00	Telephoning, letter writing, general contact with others.
12:00 – 1:30	Luncheon (alone or with friends).
1:30 – 3:30	Open.
3:30 – 4:30	Welcome kids home from school.
4:30 – 5:00	Initial dinner preparations.
5:00 – 5:30	Open – relax with husband.
5:30 – 6:00	Dinner preparations.
6:00 – 6:30	Dinner.
6:30 – 7:30	Time with husband (talking together, doing dishes together).
7:30 – 10:00	Open.

"Standard weeks" usually include standard days with variations. For example, an executive or housewife will normally do something differently on Saturday and Sunday. Certain days will be open for creative work, for training others in new tasks, or for more unscheduled time. Some people discover that Friday is a good day to "slow down"

158

and they avoid scheduling high pressure work on Fridays. (see ENERGY and KNOW YOURSELF)

Some people are in a profession or have a lifestyle which requires a standard month. People in the accounting profession, people in sales, or people who travel a great deal may find that a standard month is useful.

Pre-patterned days, weeks, months, years help operationalize a lifestyle uniquely our own. By thus defining our standard day, week, or month and sharing it with others we make it possible for them to better fit their lifestyle into ours and to understand us better. (see LIFESTYLE and IF YOU ONLY UNDERSTOOD)

STATUS QUO

If there ever was a time-waster it's struggling to maintain the status quo. Almost by definition, status quo is what things shouldn't be. Organizations change, families change, we change. Stability is for systems, not people. People grow and develop, and change. In the people business we need to be continually reexamining who we are and what we are doing. "Status quo" thinking not only blocks creativity, but it eats up time, counteracting the processes of renewal and growth. Organizations are formed primarily to achieve goals. Like Kleenex, they should be disposable when their utility is gone.

Almost every organization ought to have a self-destruct date in which it will go out of business. With such a planned terminal date the worst thing that can happen would be that it would have to reaffirm its charter. The best thing that could happen would be that people would have an opportunity to gracefully bow out of something they should have stopped doing weeks, months or years ago.

Businesses are learning the value of "budgeting from zero" each period. The individual can benefit from a similar approach. Periodically, reevaluate *everything* you are doing. Start from zero in allocating your time and resources to the achievement of your goals. Rigidly confine the plusing and minusing of readjustments to the period in-between.

STAY AHEAD OF YOUR WORK

Have you ever noticed that it is the busy people who oftentimes seem to have time to take on more tasks? One of the keys to their success is that they finish their tasks or the major portion of them *ahead* of time and thus leave themselves slack time in which they can either find relief (see RELIEF VALVES) or help out other people. (see TIME FOR OTHERS)

This technique takes awhile to learn. When I went to seminary at the ripe age of 40 I already had 17 years of experience of managing myself and others. To me it seemed like the most obvious thing in the world was to find out how much work I had to do (number of pages to be read, number of papers to be written, number of class hours to be attended, etc.) and then lay out a schedule as to when each book would be read, paper would be written and class would be attended. Knowing that most of life is failure (see FAILURE), I then tightened up my schedule so that each day's, week's, and month's work was scheduled for completion 10 percent sooner than it was needed. Meanwhile, my fellow students (most of whom were considerably younger than I) were busily involved getting themselves occupied with outside activities, new projects, and interesting discussions. The results were predictable. When the time for final examinations arrived, they were burning the midnight oil and I was ready (albeit with some considerable anxiety!) for finals.

Try maintaining two schedules: the first to display when the task *must be done;* the second when we intend

160

to complete it. If the latter is always sometime before the former, we will discover we not only get more things done, but that there are fewer pressures on us.

T

TASKS VS. FUNCTIONS

Every organization is formed in response to perceived need. The goal of the organization and the people in it is to meet the need, sometimes for altruistic reasons, sometimes for quite selfish ones. As organizations grow, work tends to be channeled into specialties. Those who have a special competence in manufacturing, administration, accounting, teaching or selling band together in functional units centered around their mutual interests in the specialty. The trouble is that the more efficient they become in carrying out their specialized function, the more likely they are to forget the organization's primary task. This is particularly true of non-profit and volunteer organizations where the primary task is not under constant testing in a market. Christian education classes in churches, PTA's in schools, or departments of this or that can become better and better at what they are doing, which may or may not relate to their task, and drift further and further from accomplishing the goals of the parent organization.

The way out of this dilemma is always to *attempt* to build suborganizations around broader goals, objectives, and tasks. This not only keeps the emphasis where it be-

163

longs, but it assumes that when the task is completed (see CLOSURE), those involved will be encouraged to move on to the excitement of a new *organization* task, rather than continue to justify their existence by maintaining the institution to serve functional, specialist and self-goals alone.

Organizing around functions is useful if you do *not* staff and operate them in a functional mode. If functional continuity and autonomy becomes more important than task accomplishment (and they will if you stress operating functionally), you had best reorganize around tasks.

TV

I have yet to see a book on managing your time that talks about television. When we consider the fact that the average American adult is supposed to watch more than twenty hours of television per week, this seems to me to be a major omission.

Some of the greatest times in our home have been when the television set has been out of repair (though I admit we did have trouble keeping the kids from sneaking next door to watch it there). But with such a large block of our time devoted to the boob tube, television viewing seems a prime candidate for time management.

On the good side, television can be entertaining, relaxing and informing. For the tired executive who needs to become engrossed in something entirely different, the Saturday afternoon football game may be just the ticket (although going to the local high school game may be healthier). For the busy housewife a couple of half hours of soap operas may bring the same type of emotional relief. And for children sick in bed, TV is a great babysitter.

On the negative side, television takes an exorbitant amount of time which could be invested in many other areas. It over-entertains us to the point of saturation. It dulls our senses and warps our view of life. It keeps us away from friends, books, and stimulating ideas.

What should be done? Certainly we should have a schedule for each member of our families (including ourselves!) on how much TV exposure we are going to tolerate a week. This might involve us in a family conference to select those programs that the family or individuals would watch during the week. It might call for a frank discussion between husband and wife as to whether the Saturday afternoon football game for him is better than bike riding in the park for both of them. It might mean the searching out of educational or particularly outstanding programs so that these become events in the individual's or family's life. It might mean getting rid of the thing entirely.

With the advent of cassette players for TV sets there is little doubt that television will offer tremendous potential for training and cultural enrichment. But for the family who has been trained to accept the average, low-vitamin fare served by TV daily, it will be a whole new way of life and one for which they may not be ready.

THANK YOU

One of the best long-term investments in effective time management is a well placed "thank you." It seems as if it's almost impossible to bank too much of this kind of currency.

As Thomas Harris* and others have pointed out, we need to know we are recognized by others as having made a contribution to our group. We need to be affirmed as individuals in the role we are playing.

If you tend to be a problem solver (as I do) you may be emphasizing needed improvements rather than past

---

*Thomas Harris, I'm O.K., You're O.K.

accomplishments. This kind of emphasis too often fills up so much of our view of the world that we forget to be grateful, both to others and to God, for all the good things.

A daily routine of identifying a task well done with a resulting note, phone call, or personal word of commendation will open up communication channels and build strong bridges toward future relationships.

THINGS ARE AS THEY ARE

Many years ago, shortly after I was first made a leader of my engineering group, one of my young associates and I were deep in a technical discussion. We were both frustrated by our inability to reach agreement. In the heat of the technical argument he blurted out, "Well, you have to admit that things *are* as they are!"

What a ridiculous argument—or so it seemed at the time.

But what a basic truth. Failure to admit that things are as they are leads to all kinds of inappropriate behavior and some very inappropriate plans.

When we are goal-setting and trying to build images of what the future might be like, we need to forget about where we are right now. But when it comes to constructing the planning bridge between things as we want them to be and things as they are now, we had best face up to the reality that surrounds us.

Too often we keep acting on the assumption that people or things have not changed because we have not, or that people always do what they say they will. Or that we have reached one step toward our goal (and are ready to move toward the next step) just because the calendar we marked said we should have.

One interesting result of failing to admit things are as they are is assuming that the *potential* in people already exists in being. Many times we bring people into an organization because they have "potential" and then we fail to give them the training or the time to develop that potential.

Another variation of this is assuming people have adequate information and have accepted our goals as theirs. The result is that they are unable to help us change the things that are as they are.

THINGS-TO-DO LIST

An effective way of getting your day, week, or month in order is continually to jot down a list of "things to do." Some people need only the back of an envelope or a torn-out sheet from a note pad. Others like a more formal system including lists of *kinds* of things to do such as phone calls to make, people to see, items to buy, letters to write, tasks to be done.

Writing down such a list accomplishes a number of things. First, it shows you what lies ahead and helps you to straighten out your priorities. Second, it helps you to get your day, week, or month in order and to visualize mentally the task that lies ahead. Third, it helps you see the interrelationship between different things, many times leading you to accomplish more than one thing at the same time. (see TWO TIMERS) Fourth, it relieves you of the conscious or subconscious worry that accompanies trying to remember to do something — a very freeing experience. Fifth, it gives you a sense of accomplishment and closure as you cross things off through the day or week.

Some appointment book and calendar systems have a place to write down "things to do" next to each day of the week. This is particularly useful, as you remember something that needs to be done, you can put it down next to the *day* in which you intend to do it.

Other people find it convenient to carry a note pad or just 3 x 5 cards on which they can jot down things to do as they remember them through the day.

Beginning each day and week by compiling such a list can change your life dramatically.

THREE-BY-FIVE CARDS

It's amazing how one small tool can change a society. The ballpoint pen has changed the whole office forms industry. It has also revolutionized the entire process of writing and put a great many pencil-makers out of business.

The three-by-five card may not be as an important invention as the ballpoint pen, but it certainly has a lot going for it. Carrying around three-by-five cards in your pocketbook, billfold, or appointment book can do the following:

— Provide a place to write *reminders* to yourself of things to be done. I used to carry just one 3 x 5 card in my breast pocket on which I would scribble in minute handwriting any thought or idea that came to my mind. I only put down enough to jog my memory. ("Enough" seems to grow with age.) At the beginning of each day I would review the card and cross off those things which I had done and review the other things which had yet to be done. When the card was filled-up, I would transfer the things yet undone to another one and begin all over again. The beauty of this system is that you always have a place to put an idea regardless of what time it hits you. (see WRITE IT DOWN)

— Provide ready-made *notes* to be sent to others. This can save a lot of time but means you may have to carry quite a few cards around.

— Provide a convenient form on which to make a quick *check list* for planning or meeting agendas. Getting into the habit of always pulling out a 3 x 5 card and making a few notes is an ideal way to get your thoughts together before you plunge into discussion. (see MEETINGS — INFORMAL)

— Provide an excellent *file* organizer. As ideas come to mind you can put a title on the card and then file it alphabetically by subject or idea for future use. This is particularly useful for those people who are involved in creative writing or in preparation of sermons and speeches.

— Provide direct access to a tickler file. (see TICKLER FILE) By writing a note to yourself and putting a date on it you can then store it in a 3 x 5 card box arranged according to the date the things involved should be done. (And 3 x 5 cards also make excellent paper airplanes for would-be aeronautical engineers.) Note: 3 x 5 cards are expensive. In this ecological age of recycling etc., consider other sources of supply. Many printing houses sell paper that was printed on one side and then not used. They bind these into cheap note pads. Many stationers carry similarly inexpensive bound or unbound slips. I personally find it convenient to standardize on one size—hence, "3 x 5".

THE TRADITION OF CHANGE

Traditions are good. They point out to us *tried and true* methods of carrying out tasks. They provide patterns of progress within which we can see ourselves working. They permit people to share expectations and to feel comfortable with each other. There are all kinds of traditions. In one sense they are nothing more than "consensus habits" which everyone has agreed to employ.

Traditions are also bad. They go out of style, sometimes very rapidly. The story is told of an analysis that was made of a British artillery crew during the Battle of

Britain. The five were firing a field gun of World War I vintage. Just before the lanyard was pulled, two of the crew snapped to attention and stood rigidly behind the gun. When asked why they did this, no one was quite sure. Eventually a retired general who had fought in the Boer War uncovered the reason. The tradition went back to the days when the guns had been *horse*-drawn. The two men standing at attention were holding the horses!

What we really need for each individual and organization is a *tradition of change*. Make it part of your lifestyle that something in you each year is going to change to keep pace with the changing situation within which you are working. (see KILL IT!)

TICKLER FILE

A tickler file is not a nail file with a feather glued on the end of it. But it is very effective way of saving time by calling to our attention those things which need to be done at the right time. Sometimes it is called pending files.

There are many variations of tickler files. Perhaps the easiest to understand is one which uses 3 x 5 cards. A 3 x 5 card file box is set up with monthly, and sometimes daily, dividers. When there is need to be reminded to take an action on a given day, the *action* to be taken is written on the face of the card, and the *date* on which the action should be recalled to mind is placed in the upper right hand corner of the card. The *name* of the individual who should take the action is placed in the upper left hand corner of the card. The card is then filed in the card file box under the date on which it should be *recalled*. Each day the individual responsible looks in the tickler file to see if there are any events which should be called to someone's attention on that day.

In addition to writing just one card for the day of the event, a "warning" card can be inserted for some appropriate time in advance. For example, if on November 21 you plan a Christmas party that is to take place on December 21, you might want to put something in the file for November 14 with the reminder: "Start thinking about plans for Christmas party planning meeting."

There are many advantages of the tickler file:
— It permits a large number of people to store reminders in one place where they can be recalled by one person.
— It permits ideas for the future to be stored away until a more appropriate time and this keeps them from being lost.
— It permits recurring projects, such as the need to write weekly reports, to be scheduled in week after week or month after month.
— It builds up a history of what has gone before and gives us a diary of the events of the past year which helps us to plan the year ahead.

Some executives use a carbon copy of a letter they have written for a pending file. They put down the date on which they should follow up and then have a file in which they keep such letters arranged by the date in which they would like to recall them. This is another version of the same system.

Tickler files not only help you organize your work and thus save time, but they thus remove all the mental pressure of having to remember what has to be done next.

Find your own system. It really works!

Note: Tickler files can supplement — or replace — calendars, or vice versa. (see PROVERBS) If you use both, be sure they are coordinated.

TIME FOR OTHERS

All of life is a series of relationships. Few people would find any satisfaction if they had to live life alone. Our greatest enjoyment comes in being able to share joys and sorrows, experiences and ideas with other people. Paul caught the ideal so well: "If one member suffers, all suffer together, if one member is honored, all rejoice."

But with the extreme mobility of our Western society and the growing number of demands on our time and the ever-multiplying number of distractions (and attractions!) that crowd into our lives, our relationships can become shallow, unsatisfying, and ineffective. This is true in both the public and private sectors of our lives.

At the business level it takes its form in the man who is so busy that for him every meeting or personal discussion is an obstacle to progess. He lives so much for tomorrow and next month, and the job that "has to be done" next week, that time with other people becomes an irritation. His associates quickly sense this and either avoid him or become irritated with him. This only serves to enforce his feelings about his work and people. Consequently, few if any of his associates ever learn to understand him *as a person*. They may respect him, even admire him, but they really don't *know* him. As a result, barriers to communication and ineffective team work keep getting in the way.

In the private area of our lives the same phenomenon can occur. Acquaintances and casual friendships multiply rapidly. Most of us find many people with whom we can have a pleasant conversation at a church meeting or at a party. There may be neighbors with whom we have casual friendships. Just living in the same place for a number of years gives us a sense of "being known" and, therefore, can give us a false sense of having many friends. But most of us need a few deeper relationships. We need those one or two other couples or two or three individuals with whom we feel we can really express ourselves freely, who will accept us just as we are, and to whom we can take our inner problems. And we need to feel there are others who view us the same way. (see ACCOUNTABILITY)

Most business relationships are easier to build than close personal relationships for the simple reason that we spend much more time in our occupational situation than we do with our nonprofessional friends. But both take time and both are worth the investment.

This means having enough flexibility so that we can take time to build these relationships. (see STAY AHEAD!) One way of doing this is to have two different types of planned encounters, one in which you report or have people report to you, and the other, just open time to discuss problems. Such times can be built into a standard week. (see STANDARD MONTH, WEEK AND DAY) Then there should also be open blocks of time which you are going to let others fill up as their needs for time with you occur. However, some people will just not take advantage of this type of situation. You will have to seek them out. This means that on your analysis of your own time (see INVENTORY) you will have to insure that you are getting a balance, and some associates aren't taking more time than they should.

Review your calendar with your wife and find out what kind of friends you really have and how much time you are spending with them. Another way of getting at this is to draw a series of concentric circles. Place your name in the center circle and then in that same circle put the names of very close or intimate friends. In the next circle put the names of close friends. In the next circle put the names of casual friends and so on. This will give you some idea of how many in-depth relationships you really have.

It takes time to build friendships. Younger people are much more adept at getting down to meaningful subjects quickly. But stake out a claim on those people into whose lives you think you can really build and who could build into your life. Then set about building these close relationships. Put aside time to do this and protect it jealously. It's the basis of living.

TIME-WASTERS

Lack of PURPOSE _____

Undefined GOALS _____

Failure to use FAILURE _____

Lack of PRIORITIES _____

Accepting jobs you can't do (see
    KILL IT and DELEGATION) _____

Unbalanced LIFESTYLE _____

Misconception of WORK — what is it? _____

Forgetting the LITTLE THINGS _____

Tackling the wrong job at the wrong
    time (see SCHEDULING) _____

Forgetting the A, B, C's _____

PROCRASTINATION _____

Lack of organization (see ORGANIZING) _____

Lack of schedule (see SCHEDULING) _____

Misunderstanding of GIFTS _____

Shuffling papers (see MAIL) _____

Poor TIMING _____

FIRE FIGHTING _____

TOO MUCH TIME to do the job (see CLOSURE) _____

Too little time to do the job (see PLANNING) _____

INTERRUPTIONS _____

Poor instructions (see DELEGATION) _____

Ignorance (see LEARNING) _____

DELEGATION _____

TELEPHONE CALLS _____

PROCRASTINATION _____

TELEVISION _____

Not enough ENERGY _____

Poor HABITS _____

Over planning (see PLANNING —
    HOW TO DO IT) _____

Failure to have ALTERNATE PLANS _____

Failure to FOLLOW UP _____

TIME — WHAT IS IT?

Time is the most valuable resource we have. In fact, in one sense, it's all we have. To each man is given only one life. In any given day each one of us has the same amount of time.

Therefore we should be more concerned with the *quality* of time than we are with the quantity of it.

Time is really nothing more than a rhythm of events. Early man measured time by the rising of the sun or the moon. Modern man measures time with the use of atomic clocks. But whether it be the rising of the sun or the motion of the atom, it is still event upon event.

There are good times and bad times, the best of times, and the worst of times. Time is neither storable nor retrievable, loanable or borrowable. It accrues and must be spent. The question is how we will spend it, how will we invest that which has been given to us?

Time becomes more and more important as we move into industrialized societies. Time may hang heavily on the hands of the village dweller in India. For the city dweller in urban America, time may be in extremely short supply. The reason for this is that an industrial society demands that we synchronize our time with the time of others. The need for accurate time-keeping becomes more important as we intersect other people or intersect each other's tasks. If the train won't leave until we get there, keeping close track of time is not important. If, on the other hand, we know the train will leave precisely when it is scheduled to leave, then keeping time is very important.

The view of time varies in different cultures. In one society being five minutes late for an appointment may require an explanation. In another society one may arrive one hour late and not be expected to give an excuse.

Time therefore becomes more and more relational. If we see it this way, we will realize that good time management in a modern society insists we manage both our "unplanned" time as well as our planned time.

Another way of looking at time is in terms of how much of our personal time we actually control, how much of it is actually discretionary time. If we are committed to an 8 to 5 job on an assembly line, there is no sense in talking about "managing our time" during that 8 to 5 period (with exception of breaks and lunch hours). All of our time is controlled by our superiors.

This might easily lead us into thinking that if we are in some "management" role we have unlimited discretionary time. Most good managers know this is not the case. They not only have time which is demanded of them by their superiors, but they also have time which is required of them by their subordinates. So time on the job may be divided into:

— Superior imposed time

— Subordinate and peer imposed time

— Discretionary time

See how much you have of each, and relate it to your goals.

TIMING

A good idea is only useful if it's introduced at the right time.

There's nothing more frustrating than a person who is loaded with good ideas and creative suggestions which neither he nor his organization can implement because of current financial or time limitations.

The same is true of the timing of decisions, it's almost as frustrating to have a decision made too early — or too late!

At the same time there's nothing more valuable than a rather commonplace suggestion or a rather uninspired decision placed at *exactly* the right time.

176

Before suggesting a new approach or deciding on a solution, check the timing.

Will this idea or action be:

— Understood now?

— Useful now?

— Accepted now?

— If not, when will it be?

> For everything there is a season, and a time for every matter under heaven:
> A time to be born, and a time to die;
> A time to plant, and a time to pluck up
> what is planted;
> A time to kill, and a time to heal;
> A time to break down, and a time to
> build up;
> A time to weep, and a time to laugh;
> A time to mourn, and a time to dance;
> A time to cast away stones, and a
> time to gather stones together;
> A time to embrace, and a time to
> refrain from embracing;
> A time to seek, and a time to lose;
> A time to keep, and a time to cast
> away;
> A time to rend, and a time to sew;
> A time to keep silence, and a time
> to speak;
> A time to love, and a time to hate;
> A time for war, and a time for peace.
>
> Ecclesiates 3:1-8 (RSV)

TOO MUCH TIME

There are some people who waste time just because they have too much of it. They just have not been given, or have not given themselves, enough goals to meet.

177

This not only wastes time at the moment but it builds in habits of idling along, habits which are hard to break when work demands suddenly build up. Too much time can be the result of a number of things:

Fuzzy goals many times immobilize people and keep them from figuring out what to do next.

Lack of information about the pending work load causes people to slow down rather than sit idle while they wait for the next assignment.

Poor *schedule analysis* can create peaks and valleys.

Improper *sequencing* of events can leave people waiting for others to complete their tasks.

Failure to delegate, or to delegate clearly, may keep people from recognizing that they *do* have work to do.

Lack of training keeps people from doing things they could do if they knew how.

Lack of closure keeps people too long on tasks, as Parkinson so discernibly states.

Overstaffing by leaders or managers who want to be prepared for the "big load" leaves people twiddling their thumbs and frustrated.

Find out where you have too much time. Uncover the source. Put that time to good use.

TRAINING

How discouraging and time-consuming it is to have to do a task we really don't know how to do. Any husband who has tried to cook for his sick wife knows the feeling.

178

Any child who has been sent on an errand that he really doesn't understand knows what I'm talking about.

On the other hand, what a pleasure it is to watch a skilled craftsman go about his job with sureness, dexterity, and *economy* of motion.

Effectiveness comes with experience, but it comes much faster if it is reinforced with training. Before tackling a job or asking someone else to do it, first ask the question, "What training is going to be needed in order for the assigned person to carry out this task?" (see DELEGATION) This may lead to the next question which is, "Could someone else do it better?"

Providing the training as part of the task will not only promote great enthusiasm, it will also get things done a lot faster.

TRIGGERS

A trigger is something which starts something else (as anyone who's ever fired a gun knows!).

Triggers are excellent ways to make or break habits (see HABITS), and to start time-saving thought processes working.

A pastor shared with me the fact that he had been unable to stop "bringing the office home" each night, and consequently was discovering he wasn't giving his family the kind of quality time they really needed. Finally he hit on a solution. He couldn't get the office out of his mind, but he could fill up his mind with his family and their needs as he drove home. Each night as he made a turn off the freeway about two miles from his home, he started thinking about each member of his family — what they might have done that day, what their needs would be, what kinds of questions they might be asking. The trigger was that turn off the freeway and continually repeating it he used the occasion to start his mental processes going.

Behavorial scientists tell us that environmental triggers such as this are very powerful tools, and we need to look for similar clues around us not only to see what's triggering our bad habits, but also what could trigger good ones. (see HABITS)

Clearing the agenda is also vital. (see CLOSURE) Triggers should not face competition they cannot beat!

In addition to looking for triggers that you might find in your own life, environment or within yourself, it is possible to create them in your life situation. One way of doing this is to share what it is you want to accomplish with your friends, family, a secretary, or associates, and ask them to call you to account when the appropriate situation arises. (see ACCOUNTABILITY)

Gentle rewards and penalties are very effective here. Perhaps you would like to use the supper hour as a time for family sharing of events. You challenge the family to spend the entire supper hour discussing only what they have done during the day. A dollar bill placed on the table at the beginning of dinner might indicate that if you all stay with it through the meal, that dollar would be invested toward going out to dinner at your favorite restaurant when you have enough dollars.

Think of different ways in which you can build in a conditioned response to a situation. These are the triggers which will help to rid yourself of bad habits and encourage new good ones.

TRIPS

Most people who don't do a great deal of traveling, wish they did. Those who do a lot of traveling, wish they didn't. How many executives have been to a hundred cities around the country or around the world and have seen little more than the airport, a hotel, and one place of business or a church? Trips take large blocks of time, but that time can be used creatively and effectively if a little planning is done ahead of time.

Have an agenda and a goal for your trip. If possible, have more than one goal.
- What other things can you be doing while you're on this trip?
- Could you make a short side trip that would cover another goal?
- Are there people whom you should call on the phone while you're in a particular city or waiting at the airport? Make up a list ahead of time.

Create a check list for the trip. (see CHECK LIST) Perhaps you need a standard check list for all of the things you normally will need.

Create a home check list, too. What needs to be done while you're away? What problems will come up at the office or home? Do you want any mail forwarded? What kind? Who will handle your mail and how is it to be answered while you're gone?

Set up trip folders for the cities you'll visit, and file in advance those things you'll need in each place.

Plan reading and writing that you will do. Usually you can be assured you'll have all the privacy you want in an airplane seat, and a three-hour flight may provide you with more space to yourself than you'll get any other time during the month! A small cassette recorder is a big help here.

Keep a file on "trip reading," material you don't have time for right now — books, pamphlets, or magazines you "always wanted to read."

Carry stamped self-addressed envelopes to mail notes home and to the office. (They'll miss you too!)

Take time to really see something besides what you would normally see on your "business."

Take your wife (or son or daughter) along with you, and schedule your trips close to vacation time. There are all kinds of alternate airline routes that cost little extra. And if you can't take your wife, make certain she and your secretary have a detailed itinerary of transportation schedules, phone numbers and addresses where you'll be staying and people you'll be with. You'll feel more comfortable knowing you *can* be reached if needed, and so will they.

On long or extended trips make sure you give yourself a "break." (see KNOW YOURSELF) Avoid *too* many hospitality visits and try to schedule them where they'll do the most good. The money you save staying with friends may cost you considerably in well-being.

TWO-TIMERS

There are a number of situations in which we can do more than one thing at the same time. By identifying these we can not only improve our efficiency, but also get rid of some of our frustrations.

If you do a great deal of automobile driving, there are a number of things you can do besides listen to the radio. Taking along a cassette recorder permits you to listen to training or inspirational tapes you might not have had the time for otherwise. It also permits you to do some dictation while you are driving. Just make sure you have a clip-on microphone so that your hands are free!

Another two-timer for automobile driving is memorizing material. This is particularly true if you are going to be doing a lot of stop-and-go driving and can refer back to whatever it is you are trying to memorize. I can remember one time when I drove 15 minutes to work each day during which time I encountered a number of stop-lights. I managed to memorize four verses of scripture a day by the simple expedient of having my New Testament lying on the seat beside me. (I actually looked forward to stop-lights so I could sneak a look at the text.)

If you are faced with a long stretch of uninterrupted driving, this is a good time to think through problems. Before you leave jot down on a 3 x 5 card some of the major questions you need to think through and talk to yourself about.

If you have a regular program of recreation or exercise, such as jogging, golf or bowling, this is a good time to combine thinking with fellowship with friends or time for making new ones.

Walking the dog is usually a lonely task, but it's an ideal time to arrange the day ahead. The same is true of jogging.

If you must take a business trip, see if you can arrange it to coincide with a useful vacation trip. (see TRIPS)

If you have to be out of the work situation for any extended period of time, take your wife along with you overnight. It will do her a world of good, and it certainly alleviates loneliness in the evenings.

If you are in a situation in which you may have to do considerable waiting for people, as in offices or hospitals, make sure you have something with you to read. This is also a good time to do some planning. (see THREE-BY-FIVE CARDS)

We spend a lot of time getting dressed and undressed. This might be a good time also to have your cassette recorder around to listen to the things for which you would not otherwise have time.

I get some of my most brilliant ideas while shaving. In fact, I'm often grateful for a battery powered shaver that lets me continue shaving while I look for my idea list to jot them down.

A word of caution: two-timing can become compulsive. If you are one of those extremely task-oriented persons, perhaps you need to *avoid* two-timers.

U

UNEXPECTED CALLERS

In a society in which we have had to gear ourselves to preset dates and common "intersection times" on the calendar, nothing can be more delightful nor more distressing than an unexpected caller. How good it is to have friends who feel they can call upon us unannounced and be assured of our warm reception. And how distracting it is to have chronic interrupters who are always sticking their head in our office for "just a word." How do we react to unexpected callers, whether in person or on the telephone?

The first thing to do is to indicate what your situation is. If you have only five minutes, say so and indicate a time when you will have a freer moment. Be positive, not "I have only 15 minutes, Harry"; but "This is great, Harry. I have 15 minutes until my next commitment. I am glad you stopped by!"

Try to learn quickly what the real need is so that another time may be scheduled if needed. If the need can be met with a later meeting, pull out the appointment calendar and make a date right there. But recognize too that there are times when our Christian priorities *demand* the task be postponed to care for the person who has a desperate need *right now.*

Note near the end of the specified time that you'd like to sum up, or that the time is drawing to a close.

Indicate to your caller by standing up or moving toward the door that your time is gone.

I know one executive who has his secretary announce to him in the presence of the visitor that it is time for his next commitment. This permits the visitor to graciously excuse himself. (see also INTERRUPTIONS)

WE TRIED THAT ONCE AND IT DIDN'T WORK

"We tried that once and it didn't work." Maybe it wasn't the right time or perhaps the people who tried it weren't skillful. It's good to learn from failure (see FAILURE) but don't let this standard creativity-stopper keep you from finding new ways of saving time.

Some strategies for handling this ploy:

1. Find out what was tried and make your proposal clearly a contrast.

2. Find out what the situation was at the time and point out the reasons for prior failure.

3. Report the success others are having with it, especially those whose success may be significant to us.

4. Try again. And this time pay more attention to organizing and communicating ideas in ways which disarm resistance. (see THE GOLDEN BALL)

WHOLE MAN

Most books on management and time management have been written from the viewpoint of the organization. The readers of such books are people who want increased output from the individual to create a more efficient enterprise to produce a better product. Therein lies their fatal weakness. They treat individual lives as though they could be compartmentalized. They deal with work as though it is only that which is sold and purchased. If we base the task of managing time, which is really managing our life, on a concept which does not include the *whole man*, we will settle for second best. The biblical concept of a person is that all of his life is interrelated. Most important is what he *is*, not what he accomplishes. (see GOALS) More important than what he accomplishes, is how he relates to others and plays his role in relationship to others.

This is not to downgrade accomplishment at all. The zest of life is in seeing the world change. That "world" may be the small world of one's family, or the larger world of a total society. A fulfilled life is one which has made a meaningful contribution toward the whole.

Great contributions are made not only in the arena of the business or professional world, but also in the arena of a total society. Somehow we must come to believe that life must be lived wholly and completely with no essential part of it neglected. (see KNOW YOURSELF and PEOPLE) Such an understanding has great power to unleash creative talents and uncover gifts. It frees us from measuring a person's worth by his status in the organization and helps us look into the deeper areas of life. It diverts us from the "success" motive to the "being" motive. Some people make their greatest contribution to society because they have the gift of a listening ear and an understanding heart.

A "whole man" concept will also encourage leaders of organizations to design a healthy organizational environment, a place where individuals are growing in many dimensions. Since the early 60's when Douglas McGregor first postulated his Theory X and Theory Y we have gathered enough hard data to know that such a healthy organization obtains its objectives much more easily than the "this is a *business!*" approach.

WORK — WHAT IS IT?

We have some strange ideas about work. One of the first questions we may ask upon meeting someone is "what do you do?" or "where do you work?" In our mind, work is that which we are paid to do, that from which we gain a livelihood, that which produces money for us which can then be used to invest in "leisure time."

Our Western society is rapidly changing its concept of work, and rightfully so. The concept of work which implies that it must return excess income over investment for the individual is a very limiting one. Compartmentalizing life in the way we spend our time is also an ineffective use of time.

Life is given to us to give glory to God by sharing it with others. We "share" in many ways. We can share by the money or material we give or make available for others. We can share on the level of ideas. We can share just by being available and by supporting others as they work through continually reoccurring tragedies of life.

It will be probably another 10 years before our society has found a way to reorganize itself out of the eight-to-five strait-jacket. Meanwhile, the Christian has a tremendous advantage over those who stand outside the Body of Christ. Since there is a higher, over-arching purpose, and meaning to all he does, a new definition is given to the concepts of both "work" and "leisure." Of all people, the Christian should be freed to see life as a whole and to see his vocation as a calling that is no less a part of God's plans than any other part of his life.

In 1959 I left a job of eleven years with the Sperry Gyroscope Company at Great Neck, New York to move to a new position with Lear Seigler in Grand Rapids, Michigan. In 1964 I left Grand Rapids to attend Fuller Seminary in Pasadena, California. There was a tremendous contrast between the two moves, both as to short range goals and life situation (not to mention financial level). What seemed to startle my friends the most was that my family and I saw no great contrast in attending seminary or acting as an aerospace executive in terms of God's leading and directing in our lives. It is no more "spiritual" to be at a seminary or less sanctified to find life's vocation in industry.

Work is the task you are called to do. Not necessarily that for which you get paid for (in money).

WRITE IT DOWN!

The mind is a fantastic storage system. We are told that most of us use very little of our total capacity. Recent experiments indicate that all of our life experience is stored in our minds, and potentially it can be recalled in such a way we may not only remember it, but we may *experience* it.

But until we are supplied with some kind of electro-chemical memory inducer, most of us discover that as our minds are loaded with more and more incidentals. We have greater and greater difficulty remembering things we want to recall.

So carry a paper and pencil or pen wherever you are. Carry a note pad of 3 x 5 cards on which you can record things.

If you are in the middle of a meeting and you suddenly get a flash of inspiration, write it down. If you are eating dinner in a restaurant and an idea crosses your mind, write it down. If the events of the day tend to keep you awake at night (or wake you up too early in the morning), keep a pad and pencil next to your bed and write it down. Many times this will "unload" your subconscious and let you go back to sleep. If you are in the midst of a time of prayer, and you suddenly remember something that needs to be done or an idea you need to recall, stop and write it down. God may have given it to you.

Some people carry a note pad on which they can write notes to others and get rid of them the moment they think of them. Other people use their appointment book or daily calendar or a things-to-do list.

Work out your own system. Don't make it too elaborate, but have a system.

And write down things about other people. You can't love people until you really know something about them, and knowing them takes work. Gain an understanding of other people and you'll greatly reduce the time it takes to communicate with them. (see COMMUNICATION)

Y

YOUR BALL

Well, that's the tool box for managing your life by managing your time. Some of it will be exactly what you need right now. Other tools may be needed later.

Look over the table of contents and decide which ones you should put to work today, next week, next month.

It's your ball.